Jewellery Handbooks:

THE

EARRINGS

BOOK

Yvonne Kulagowski

A&C BLACK
LONDON

Daphne Krinos, *Earrings*, oval aquamarine cabochons set in 18-carat yellow gold, with three hexagonal aquamarine crystals, 2004. Photograph by Joël Degen.

First published in Great Britain in 2007
A & C Black Publishers Limited
38 Soho Square
London W1D 3HB
www.acblack.com

ISBN-13: 978-0-7136-6505-5

CIP Catalogue records for this book are available from the British Library and the U.S. Library of Congress.

Book design by Jo Tapper
Cover design by Sutchinda Rangsi Thompson
Copyedited by Paige Weber
Proofreading and indexing: Sophie Page
Project Manager: Susan Kelly

Printed and bound in China by South China

This book is produced using paper that is made from wood grown in managed, sustainable forests. It is natural, renewable and recyclable. The logging and manufacturing processes conform to the environmental regulations of the country of origin.

Contents

ACKNOWLEDGEMENTS

My grateful thanks to all 48 jewellers who have allowed me to bombard them with questions, talking to me at great length, in minute detail, about their work and for allowing me to use the wonderful images of their earrings.

Particular thanks to Barbara Christie (Chapter 5), Rachel Dorris (Chapter 3), Maria Spanou (Chapter 3) and Zoe Arnold (Chapter 1) for making and meticulously photographing the earring projects. Thanks also to Michael Taylor who has been generous with his time, reading this book in its various draft stages and offering vital critical advice.

My thanks to Central Saint Martins College of Art and Design for awarding me a research grant which allowed me to spend important time initially examining jewellery, visiting and interviewing the artists, and Camberwell College of Arts for the dedicated research time included in my teaching post that I have used to do much of the writing.

I am indebted to Linda Lambert, Susan Kelly and A&C Black for giving me this opportunity as well as their encouragement and support.

Finally I thank my dear friend Gail M. Brown who gave me the encouragement and confidence to begin my journey of discovery.

Above: Jane Adam, *Folded Earrings*, anodised, dyed aluminium and stainless steel, 2001. Photograph by Joël Degen.

Introduction

Earrings come in an infinite range of designs, styles and prices. They can be worn to suit various occasions and fit any mood or dress code – anything goes! Whether one's taste lies in one-off designs, the versatility found in production ranges or in making a statement with wild, extravagant exhibition or fashion collections, this book considers and develops these areas in depth. Using images to explain design decisions and technical details, the style and appeal of earrings will be analysed, thus putting them into context in today's growing market for the unique and unusual in a special piece of jewellery.

While all the jewellers featured aim and intend their work to be worn, the variations and interpretations of this are fascinating. Case studies explore individual 'art' pieces made for public and private clients, fashion show and catwalk collections, political and/or narrative exhibition pieces as well as 'practical' everyday earrings.

Projects show the manufacture of simple stud, hanging and complex two part drop earrings in detail. These explain and clarify design and technical decisions and share 'tips' that simplify the making process.

Research, in the main, has taken the form of interviews with the artists, talking to them about the various influences on their jewellery. Where possible, web site addresses are provided to enable the enthusiast to find out and view more of the artists' work. Lists and contact details of the main UK, European, US and Canadian galleries and trade events are included. To enable additional exploration there is a glossary of technical terms and suggested further reading lists of technical processes and studio jewellery.

Yvonne Kulagowski, 2007

Above: Vickie Sedman, *Earrings*, antler, sterling silver and 14-carat gold, L 7.6 cm, 1996.
Photograph by Vickie Sedman.

1
Getting started

The tools and equipment photographs in this chapter were taken in Zoe Arnold's workshop, by Zoe Arnold, unless otherwise stated. *Zoe Arnold delights in creating unusual treasures, beautiful curios to secretly savour, which may be tailored to embrace a favoured story or personal reflection.* Zoe Arnold, Goldsmiths' Fair 2006 catalogue, p.20. Zoe Arnold's work is discussed in detail on pp. 118-120.

It is important to organise and plan not only your time and making but also your work surroundings. How will you move around the room or area? What storage will you need? If you are working in precious materials you will also require a secure safe.

The image above shows a typical work solution, the work bench is flanked on either side by a set of drawers to the right, housing hand tools (see pp. 8 and 9), and a cupboard on the left to hold materials and measuring equipment. The surfaces of these units can be used to put larger, regularly used pieces of equipment on. The work bench itself needs to be easily tidied at the end of each stage and can quickly get cluttered, therefore it is good planning to keep this as clear as possible. Light is very important and here the bench faces a window, with an angle poise lamp to the jeweller's left.

Tools

The jeweller's "D" shaped workbench with central bench peg is a vital feature of any workshop; for a makeshift bench I have often resorted to clamping my bench peg onto an old table, which works well on a temporary basis.

Tools to manipulate metal, from left to right: round nose pliers, flat/half-round pliers, shears, parallel pliers, end cutters and flat nose pliers.

The piercing saw is another essential tool; the saw blade is held in place by tightening the screw at either end of the saw. It is good practice to place the end between the 'V' of the bench peg and push the handle, then tighten to ensure a taught blade – a blade that is not held tightly will not saw metal. The blade is put in with the teeth facing outwards, pointing down towards the handle.

TIP

If you follow the correct stages of cleaning and finishing, polishing will just be a case of 'licking' your piece with the polisher. The only way to remove scratches or dents/dips is by filing.

Files are used first to clean up a piece of work, always try to use the largest file you can, this will ensure that your work has an even finish i.e. no dips or rounded corners where they should not be, and also is faster. Shown here (L to R) are: pillar, half-round/coarse, half-round/fine, crossing, round.

Once the main filing is done you may need to access awkward areas; needle files are used for this. These can be bought in sets of six and eight. A set of eight is shown: round, pillar, triangular, joint-round edge, half-round, knife edge, crossing, and square.

Emery paper is used next, beginning with the coarser grades e.g.120 and working through 240, 400, 600, 800 to 1200.

Hammers, (L to R): horn mallet for hammering metal into shape without getting any marks on the piece, Ball Pein hammer and Warrington hammer.

TIP

First, file in one movement, top to bottom. Once the surface has been filed, turn the work round and, using a finer file, file from side to side continuing until the work is polished. This enables you to see when you have 'eradicated' the previous stage, as all the coarser marks will be removed; if you continuously file in the same direction you do not have a sense of completing each finishing stage.

Machinery

The pendant drill is a very useful piece of equipment, you may have previously encountered one being used at the dentists! The motor speed is operated by a foot pedal leaving one's hands free to hold the pendant end in one hand and your piece of work in the other, the actual motor is best hung from a hook slightly above seated head height so that the flexible shaft does not kink and get damaged.

A wide variety of filing and finishing 'bits' are available,

Various finishing mops, (L to R): steel for brushed finish, narrow felt, calico, felt, swansdown and dolly mops.

TIP

Only use each mop with one polishing compound, never mix-up the mops as this will only slow down the process.

Rolling mills are useful for various processes, metal can be rolled thinner and can have a pattern rolled onto it (see p. 64). They operate by turning a large screw (see the handle at the top), to the required thinness and then operating the side handle to roll the metal through. A good set of mills will also have ridged rollers that have corresponding square grooves. These enable round wire to be rolled down into square section wire.

The pillar drill is useful for drilling vertical holes, It operates by turning the handle on the right and lowering the moving drill into the metal/material. The chuck is designed to take a greater range of diameters from 0.2mm to large drills used in DIY.

For soldering many jewellers use a large gas cylinder as shown here, but you can improvise and use a canister and torch head, available from large hardware/kitchen stores.

Soldering equipment

It is good to have a range of soldering torch heads and nozzles to enable you to solder on a variety of scales e.g. from jewellery size to perhaps small silversmithing objects. These are designed to give a range of flame sizes.

Soldering is the process by which two edges of metal are joined together by heating and fusing with solder. For silver there are three grades of solder: hard which melts at the highest temperature for the majority of joints; medium which melts at a lower temperature, thus previous joints soldered with hard will not melt/fall apart, and easy, lowest melt, for the very last joints.

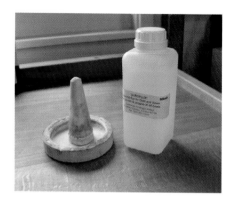

First paint the edges to be soldered with borax (on the left) or a flux (on the right) this ensures that air cannot enter the joint, allowing for successful soldering.

Soldering must be carried out in a safe environment. Here a special soldering tray accommodates a soldering turntable with a series of soldering blocks to support the piece. Note the pair of spring tweezers used to hold the work steady.

Once soldered the metal must be cleaned of residue or 'pickled'. Zoe uses safety pickle which comes in a powder and is dissolved in water. The solution is heated to a warm temperature as this quickens the process. Zoe uses an electric pressure cooker with a glass dish inside to hold the pickling solution. This way she can control the temperature and work in a clean and safe environment.

TIP

Put the solder strip through the rolling mills, this makes it easier to cut pallions by cutting up the strip and then across, to get lots of even squares of solder.

Metals, materials and precious stones

When designing jewellery it is good to be aware of what is available and make decisions accordingly. The most commonly used forms of metal are sheet and wire, sheet comes in whatever size you require and varying thicknesses. Wire can be round, square, oval and many manufacturers will produce wire to your requirements for an additional charge.

Rod or tubing (chenir) can be ordered in a variety of outer and inner diameters as well as wall thicknesses. See Amanda Doughty's earrings using chenir on p. 21.

Photograph below by Louise O'Neill

Here the jeweller chooses from a selection of diamonds; raw diamonds from the Congo, yellow and brown diamonds in various different weights, brilliant and hand cuts.

Photograph below by Louise O'Neill

The variety of choice and array of stones is almost infinite; the pink,violet, turquoise and green tourmalines are a selection of the range of natural colours that this stone has. The marquise, baguette and square cuts show the stones off to best advantage.

Inspiration

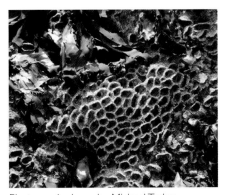

Nature is another great source of inspiration, whether it is landscape as here or close-up details of flowers and foliage.

Photograph above by Michael Taylor

Natural pattern and design, once caught as a photograph and cropped, become something quite different and exciting.

Photograph above and below by Michael Taylor

Photograph above by Michael Taylor

Detail can be taken and developed into a personal and original design idea.

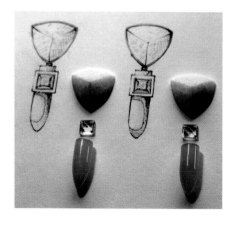

Here Barbara Christie lays out her stone combination ideas alongside her design drawings, once she is satisfied she will commence making the earrings, see Chapter 5 for the step-by-step making of this pair of earrings.

Drawing and design development

Often jewellers will be commissioned to make earrings for a special occasion such as a wedding. Here the jeweller has begun her design process with this stylisation of the pattern that appears on the bride's dress material.

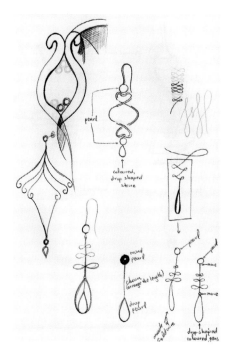

Here Maria Spanou begins to develop her design in terms of construction and material decisions.

> **TIP**
> *Always be sensible and work within your technical abilities – never show the client ideas that you are not sure about being able to fulfill as they will be sure to select that design!*

Now she must consider stones and which colours her client, the bride, will be happy with.

The final image of the finished earrings.

TIP

Never assume the client understands what you are proposing to make for them, they may just be being polite. Always provide the client with drawings, photographs of similar pieces and if you are worried then make a prototype in cheaper materials.

2
Design thoughts and processes

How much attention do we pay to the design and the intentions of the artist when looking at or wearing a particular pair of earrings? Many studio jewellers make a point of using specific metals and materials to enable their designs to explore ideas and techniques. It can be this, as well as the subject matter, that can provoke a train of thought and lead to decisions that produce an original and exciting piece of jewellery. Teaching, whether on practical or theoretical subjects, is for many jewellers a rewarding experience, entailing passing on knowledge and expertise, and presenting studio jewellery as a subject in its own right. Many of the artists in this book hold positions at a number of prominent art schools and universities in the UK and the USA, and are responsible in a variety of ways for shaping and encouraging the next generation of jewellers.

VICKIE SEDMAN is Professor of Crafts at the Tyler School of Art in Philadelphia, USA. She balances her position of educator with that of artist jeweller, the former influences the latter.

In this image (right) Sedman used deer antler, an ivory substitute, and carved it to emphasize the sensuous, curving form, which is embellished with silver and gold pods. To answer issues of wearability, Sedman reduced the weight by hollowing out the reverse of the antler, creating intrigue as to what the material is – carved, solid or formed sheet? The little pods are pressed and therefore hollow. As with the antler, they are concave and very light. It is this attention to detail that is so

Right:: Vickie Sedman, *Earrings*, antler, sterling silver and 14-carat gold, L 7.6 cm, 1996. Photograph by Vickie Sedman.

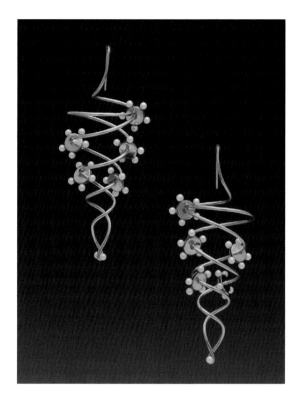

Left: Vickie Sedman, *Earrings*, 14-carat gold and pearls, L 6.4 cm, 2001.
Photograph by Vickie Sedman.

interesting. Balance and proportion have been carefully considered, along with Sedman's concerns about wearability and aesthetic judgement. The earrings move gently and light catches the metal, adding to the wearing experience. One of her aims is to design earrings with visual impact and drama, while using minimal amounts of material and weight.

Colour for the most part is not apparent. Only precious metals and varying shades of white are used. In this image (above), pearls concentrate and control the viewer's attention, moving the eye over and around the subtle aspects of the design. This light, fluid, three-dimensional form sits well in relationship to the face, ear, neck and body, emphasizing the fundamental issues of adornment and ornament. Sedman's earrings enhance the wearer, thus giving enjoyment and confidence. The ear fitting is a 'natural' continuation of the spiralling linear design at the top of the earring, as is the placing of the pearl at the base, secured by the gold wires at point of encounter.

The earring shown on p.20 is a good example of Sedman's ability to

Left: Vickie Sedman, *Earrings*, 14-carat gold and pearls, L 6.4 cm, 1999.
Photograph by Vickie Sedman.

turn a design solution into a feature of interest. Here the ear post and backing are of equal importance as the lower part, to give a sophisticated and unusual pair of earrings designed to show a continuous rod of gold passing through the ear lobe. Simplicity of manufacture and material usage is important. The upper part is scattered with small pearls, while the lower, longer length is left plain and is completed at the base with a large and small pearl combination. Jewellery at this level involves and educates the wearer, making interaction with a sophisticated pair of earrings an exciting experience.

Wearability will always be discussed. After rings and the intricacies of finger fittings, earrings are perhaps the other main item of jewellery that must sit or hang in a certain way on the ear lobe or, in certain designs, around and over the ear. Whether you are using a clip, stud or hook fitting, weight and scale must be taken into account, and of course, so must the occasion.

How wearable do earrings need to be? **AMANDA DOUGHTY** intends her earrings to be worn every day and everywhere, which is the driving force behind her design process. Her jewellery has a timeless quality; it complements rather than competes, and is all about understatement and observation. By using recognizable 'classic' forms such as circles and ovals, she places a diamond at a focal point, making her design satisfying

Above: Amanda Doughty, *Four Single Earrings*, 18-carat yellow gold and diamonds, 2003. Photograph by Richard Stroud.

and memorable. 18-carat yellow gold is used in the four earrings shown above. Earrings 1 and 2 (from the left) are made from chenier (tubing), while earrings 3 and 4 are castings of Doughty's designs.

On initial observation, the mechanics of the design appear simple. However, with closer inspection, one can see that when worn the diamonds, set at both ends of the length of chenier, are seen and admired by the viewer, not the wearer! For Doughty, using diamonds with precious metals means that she is offering a very desirable product, enabling her to move away from making production earrings to one-off and limited edition work.

The earrings below clearly show the very graphic approach that Doughty takes to designing, whether she incorporates diamonds or relies only on the form she has created in gold. This simplicity and strength is

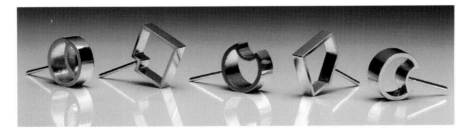

Above: Amanda Doughty, *Five Single Earrings*, sterling silver with gold tint, 2002. Photograph by Richard Stroud.

part of the appeal, along with attention to detail and little unexpected twists in the way we view ourselves, and how we wear jewellery on our ears. Doughty takes a circle and square and, by making slight modifications in the frame structures, produces totally different earrings. Basic considerations, such as the positioning of the ear post, gives the middle earring a very different look when worn from the one on the far right. This is what Doughty excels at – this intense exploration of a simple structure, from which she manages to extract an almost unlimited range of designs.

An artist's culture can play an important part in his or her design decisions. Although the majority of the jewellers featured in this book live and work in the UK, many have not been brought up there, but chose to study at UK colleges and stay, contributing to the rich cultural diversity of British studio jewellery.

KAYO SAITO readily acknowledges the links between her jewellery and her Japanese upbringing. Japanese culture has a strong tradition of paper products such as scrolls, lanterns and screens. While doing her MA at the Royal College of Art, London, she researched paper alternatives and discovered a paperlike material, a mix of plastic fibres and polyester,

which was very durable yet had the visual appeal of paper. Using this lightweight material in her jewellery, she challenges herself to work on a larger scale to produce seemingly delicate work, which is actually very robust.

In the image shown (left), a double layer of thin material is used for this unit, complimented by a central pearl, which is protected by the concave form. Light passes through the single diaphanous

Left: Kayo Saito, *Bouquet Brooch and Earrings*, polyester fibre, resin, magnets and freshwater pearls, dia. earrings 2 cm, 2003. Photograph by Kayo Saito.

Right:: Kayo Saito, *Snow Gold Brooch and Earrings*, 18-carat yellow gold, dia. earrings 3.5cm, 2003. Photograph by Kayo Saito.

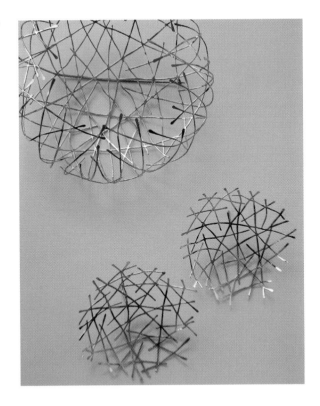

layers of the earrings and brooch, conveying feelings of delicacy and fragility. The lustrous pearls add to this, conveying a feeling of preciousness.

Saito sells through a selection of galleries in the UK, Europe and the USA; many of her customers have careers in or links with the art and design world and purchase her jewellery for private viewings and special events. The work shown above takes inspiration from the natural world, in this case snowflakes, which she stylizes into exquisite pieces of jewellery. Using a series of hammered 18-carat yellow gold wires, Saito pays careful attention to the composition of the piece, giving equal importance to the space between the wires and the wires themselves. The earrings are then hammered gently to introduce form into the structure. An ear post is soldered off-centre to ensure that when worn the earring does not 'tip forward'. It is interesting to compare the different edges of the earrings with those of the brooch, which Saito has turned back in on themselves so that they curl towards the centre of the piece. This subtlety is one of her strengths – it enables her to give a different feel or look to a piece without making drastic adjustments. This thinking extends to the choice she offers of one-off pieces, limited editions and small production runs, making sure that there is something for every customer's price range.

The Danish system of doing a four-year apprenticeship in a prestigious workshop meant that **MIKALA DJØRUP** had extensive technical training, but no real opportunity to acquire design skills. Djørup decided to do a BA Honours degree in the UK to combine her technical expertise and understanding of metal with the freedom to develop her design ideas. Despite experimenting with non-precious materials, she always returns to precious metals, preferring to work with 18-carat gold and silver. Djørup uses stones, but more as a detail or comment, with a little dot here or an accent there.

Left: Mikala Djørup, *Open Layer Ear Clip*, sterling silver, 1.5 × 2 cm, 2001. Photograph by Mikala Djørup.

Djørup's designs are influenced by pattern and repetition. With this in mind, she uses multiples to create one whole item; the intention behind the work is not to let the viewer know what the surface is at first glance, then on closer inspection he or she discovers that the pattern is in fact many layers of metal. In the piece shown above she uses narrow strips of silver, hammered to make the edges uneven. These are then cut into lengths and their edges are soldered together to create a 'fan' of metal. Because of the simplicity of the technique, Djørup is able to vary the look of the earring by having longer or shorter, and narrower or wider, strips of metal, giving an intriguing three-dimensional pattern. A clip fitting is used to best support the weight of the metal, allowing the earring to sit properly on the lobe. Djørup tends to design earrings with clip fittings as her research shows that this is what her customers prefer.

Left: Mikala Djørup, *Round Gold Ear Studs*, 18-carat yellow gold and diamonds, dia. 1 cm, 2001. Photograph by Mikala Djørup.

Above, Djørup uses hammered 18-carat yellow gold strip, this time as an outer ring or frame, soldered onto a back plate housing the central setting and diamond focal point. The height of the setting is in keeping with the height of the outer ring, and while very minimal in detail, this circular form incorporates luxurious materials and when worn movement casts light and shadow across its surface.

KATY HACKNEY does not limit herself to precious metals, preferring to include alternative materials such as cellulose acetate, Formica®, plywood and enamel paint in her repertoire, giving her earrings whatever look or feel she is currently interested in. Hackney draws inspiration from a wide range of subjects and resources such as Swedish design, Victorian ironwork, garden plants and hedges, 1950s and 1960s textiles, furniture, ceramics and quirky jewellery design.

In the image shown overleaf, all of the linear plant earrings are constructed from round silver wire, bent into the different shapes using

Above: Katy Hackney, *Nature Earrings*, sterling silver and paint, 2003.
Photograph by Katy Hackney.

jewellers' pliers. The 'drawing in wire' is soldered and finally flattened by hammering. Hackney's jewellery is so well made that it deludes the viewer with its visual simplicity. She tackles intricately challenging processes with skill and expertise, producing earrings that appear uncomplicated and memorable. She does not do much drawing to work out her designs; instead, she plays around with components and parts, with one thing leading to another. Part of her development process is the desire and ability to progress ideas, seen here in the way that this work references the graphic quality of line drawing.

What comes across in Hackney's work is a feeling of chance. She likes to be controlled by what she happens upon in junk shops, reclamation yard forays and rummaging around in skips. The discovery of an old, discarded piece of cellulose acetate or Formica®, now no longer produced and therefore extinct, is given similar standing to that of a precious jewel. Hackney will hoard it, eventually selecting it for a very special piece, the value placed on the design reflecting this.

Above: Katy Hackney, *Hearts and Flowers*, plywood, 'vintage' Formica® and sterling silver, 2004. Photograph by Katy Hackney.

In this collection made in plywood and Formica®, these large stud earrings consist of two of Hackney's favourite materials, their surface pattern enhanced by the chunkiness of the layered wood. Using kitsch heart, flower and shamrock forms, she is harking back to childhood memories of kitchen work surfaces. With this jewellery, she raises the status of the material to that of a prized possession. While there is a lack of compromise about this work – a look of the Ugly Duckling – it is increasingly popular, as her enthusiastic clientele prove. They recognize this underlying beauty, the unusual use of material and colour, and most importantly, Hackney's ability to produce a quirky yet endearing pair of earrings.

The majority of studio jewellers exhibit and sell their work through a variety of outlets ranging from small specialist craft galleries and shops to large department stores. Many take part in trade fairs such as *Goldsmiths' Fair* at Goldsmiths' Hall, *Collect* at the Victoria & Albert Museum, *Pulse*, *Dazzle* and *Origin* in London, *SOFA New York* and *SOFA Chicago* in the USA. Websites make it ever easier for the customer to discover and contact the jeweller.

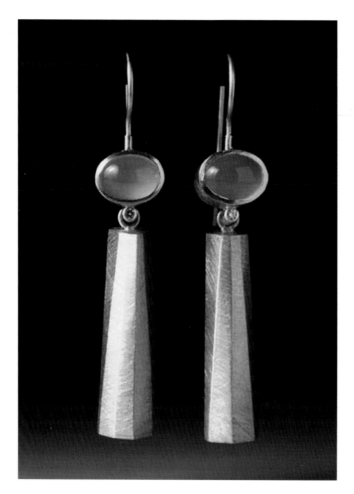

Left: Louise O'Neill, *Earrings*, 18-carat yellow gold, aquamarines and diamonds, 2003. Photograph by FXP.

LOUISE O'NEILL regularly takes part in *Goldsmiths' Fair* because it allows her to meet and speak to her clients, promoting her work through her explanation of materials and methods of manufacture. O'Neill likes to push herself technically. She enjoys the process of construction, the interplay of intersecting shapes and structure and she relishes the challenge of turning her paper models, made to test out ideas, into metal. In the earrings shown above, the large, beautiful, aquamarine cabochons are positioned to attract interest. The fabricated, 18-carat yellow gold folded form gives a contemporary yet classic feel to this elegant earring. As with all of O'Neill's work, the approach is uncluttered yet direct; a little diamond detail, a neat punctuation in the design, links top to bottom and allows movement in the lower part.

O'Neill's earrings sell consistently well. Her clientele is discerning, and much of her work is made for private commission, giving her clients the opportunity to get involved in the design process.

The stud earrings shown below use exquisite, subtle detailing of line and form, drawing the eye in towards the stones: 18-carat gold with turquoise blue and purple diamonds, and silver with green and pariba tourmalines. O'Neill offers a choice of 18-carat gold earrings with centrally positioned 18-carat gold settings, or silver earrings with 18-carat gold settings positioned at the foot, or base, of the earrings. This is a very effective use of a satin finish with this form, as light softly bounces off the angles and curves while the stones focus interest.

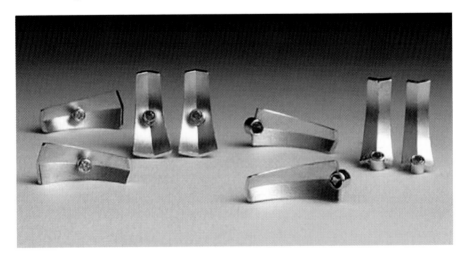

Above: Louise O'Neill, *Fold Earrings*, 18-carat yellow gold and coloured diamonds, sterling silver and tourmalines, 2003. Photograph by FXP.

Collecting studio jewellery can be rather like a treasure hunt, with one purchase or piece leading to another. The artists themselves, and the people who work in the shops and galleries that sell their work, will talk to a client about the creation of a piece of jewellery. There is so much to discover in terms of design and process, knowledge about the construction of a piece and decisions made with regard to scale, material and metal choice, as well as the artists' preference for making one-of-a-kind, limited edition or small production runs.

Left: Holly Belsher, *Silver Pod Earrings*, sterling silver and dalmation jasper, 1998. Photograph by Holly Belsher.

For **HOLLY BELSHER**, plants, leaves, pebbles and natural forms such as seed pods and flowers all inspire and contribute to the design process. Her jewellery has a very organic feel, and one can often trace the development of a design to its natural starting point. The uppermost part of the earrings shown above derived from drawings Belsher had made of pomegranates. On noticing that she had given particular emphasis to the little crown (calyx) at the top of the fruit, she then developed this into the stylized version seen here. The middle unit is square tube, heated until the edges rise up, curl and form into ridges, making the rest of the form warp and puff out, podlike, in the middle. Dalmatian jasper beads are used to complete the design. These earrings combine individually made pods with castings from original master models. As with all her earrings, Belsher reverses the upper units to give a right and a left for wearing purposes; the post or ear clip is soldered onto this part.

Belsher loves working with a material like silver, a hard metal, which she can change by heating it to its melting point. When it becomes fluid and soft like clay, it allows her to push and prod its semi-molten form as it stretches, contracts and crinkles. She confidently mixes older unit designs with more recent ones if a piece calls for it. Her work has evolved over the years, rather than changed drastically. This is what appeals to the customers who keep returning to buy more of her jewellery, adding to the pieces they already own and wear.

Above: Holly Belsher, *Twig Ear Studs*, sterling silver, natural Suffolk quartz and beach pebbles, 2004. Photograph by Holly Belsher.

The Twig Ear Studs shown above are a natural progression from looking at pods to thinking about stems and twigs as the basis of a new range of jewellery. As with many jewellers, an exhibition opportunity made Belsher finally set some time aside to explore her thoughts, observe her collection of branches and twigs and consider wire structures, another area of interest, because she wanted to design something linear. Rummaging around in Devon woods, she set about collecting the perfect twig. She found this to be a long shape with right-angled side twigs. She then made castings of the best twigs and began to play with these. By throwing them onto the floor in a heap, she was able to select random shapes and solder these together. This way of working, using resources to hand and allowing decisions to be guided by spontaneity, ties in well with the natural ethos that plays such an important part in her life.

Left: Anastasia Young, *Untitled Box Installation #14*, human and guinea-pig teeth, sterling silver, blackbird legs and mixed media, 2002. Photograph by Anastasia Young.

Often it is a mixture of things that motivates artists to think in very diverse and individual ways. For **ANASTASIA YOUNG** it is twofold: she considers both the relationship between the object and the context in which it is placed, and the technical aspects of manufacture. She uses a range of techniques, including forging, etching, fabricating and patination. These she incorporates with narrative, often presenting them in specially designed installations. Young is fascinated by the peculiar and the uncanny, her jewellery installations create an environment in which the carefully selected collection of objects can be displayed. The installation shown above, with its fascinating, mysterious, strange contents draws the viewer in to examine and ponder. The tooth earring with its' enamel, pearl-like surface and silver ear hook and attachment, is sensitively placed between key and blackbird foot. Here the earring is not just an earring but part of something else, to understand properly what is going on the viewer must look at the contents in detail.

3

Making simple earrings

Domed Stud Earrings *by Rachel Dorris*
(All photographs taken by Rachel Dorris.)
Rachel Dorris left a career in medical physics in 2003 to pursue her
dream of becoming a jewellery designer. Since then, she has built her
new career by developing a range of hand-crafted jewellery. The hollow
silver elements that characterise her work are designed to represent
natural forms such as shells, leaves and enticing crystal geodes.

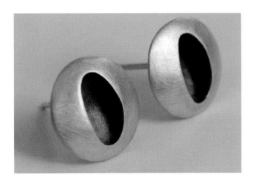

The first sequence shows
jeweller Rachel Dorris making
this pair of fabricated (hollow)
domed stud earrings. Made
from 0.5mm thick sterling
silver the outer diameter of
finished earring is 14mm.

Measuring and Planning
Dividers are used to draw-out the circular backs and fronts on the silver.

Note how Rachel is mindful of her material
waste and though keeping all her circles close
together, she allows just enough room for her
saw blade to pierce-out the circles. To pierce
out the centre of the upper circle Rachel first
uses a centre punch to mark the spot to be
drilled, then she uses the pendant drill to drill
the hole. To pierce out the central area she
must undo the saw blade and pass it through
the drilled hole, taking care not to bend the
blade as it will snap. She tightens the blade
again and pierces out the hole.

Fabricating and Soldering

Rachel now needs to anneal, or soften, the two parts of the earring before she domes and shapes them. Note how she has set up the soldering block, allowing her to heat behind as well as in front, ensuring a more consistent outcome.

The doming block is used to curve the metal into shallow domes. The side with the punch mark, used to identify the centre of the circle, is positioned so that it is on the outside and able to be used to eventually locate where the ear post will be attached.

Note: The diameter of the solid disc is reduced when domed. Rachel compensated for this and made it 1mm larger than the front disc with the pierced centre.

The edges of the two domed silver parts have been filed and sanded flat to ensure a good solder joint. The earring parts are painted with flux prior to soldering. Rachel uses the stick soldering technique. She places the earring with the largest part uppermost to enable this to be heated easily, before directing the flame evenly to the edges of the earring to encourage the solder to flow along the joint and to seal the rim.

Once the back of the earring has been cleaned to receive the post and the end of the post filed, the post can be soldered. Here Rachel uses tweezers to hold the post steady while she heats with the torch in her other hand.

TIP

Think ahead in terms of cleaning-up and easy access, emery any hammer marks on what will be the 'inside' of the earring before it is soldered.

Finishing

The earring is placed in the pickle solution and once clean is rinsed and dried before it is finished with fine-grade emery paper to ensure a neat edge and finally Scotch-brite® to give a matt finish. **Note:** the white interior finish, achieved with pickling, contrasts nicely with the matt outer.
Rachel uses the pendant drill with a strip of emery paper and split pin to clean-up the edge before burnishing.

Finally Rachel completes the earring using a burnisher to create a bright edge, this is a very effective and quick method to give detail.

Alternatives

It is a good idea to offer a choice of designs. By making a different top Rachel can easily and economically change the look and shape of the earring.

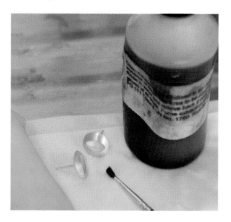

Safety: Wear rubber gloves to protect hands and goggles to protect eyes. Always work in a well ventilated area as the fumes are dangerous.

The inside of the earring is blackened or oxidised. This is done by painting on the pre-prepared oxidising solution.

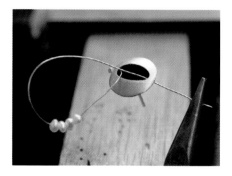

The opposing ends of the oval are carefully drilled using the pendant drill (0.6mm diameter drill). Next Rachel takes a length of 0.4mm wire, one end heated and beaded to hold in place, and a length of pearls. The wire is inserted into the first hole, the pearls threaded onto, and pulled through the second hole. It is then kinked and folded back on itself to hold it in place.

TIPS

Alternative finishes can be considered: create a bright polish inside the earring by using the pendant drill and small mop head; roll or hammer texture onto the silver surface that will be the inside of the dome; polish the outside of the earring and leave the interior matt.

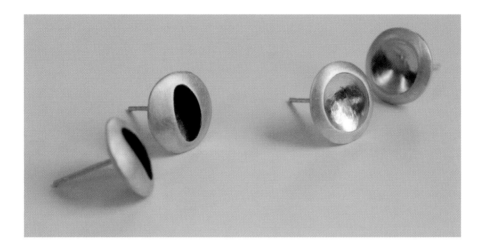

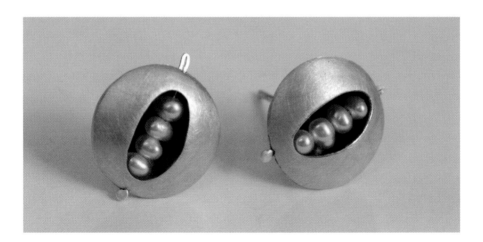

Above: Yet another alternative pair of earrings, which could open-up even more ideas by using a range of coloured beads to create yet more choice.

Wire earrings set with stones
by Maria Spanou

(All photographs taken by Maria Spanou)

Maria Spanou graduated from Central Saint Martins College of Art and Design in 2006, and currently has her workshop in South London. The beaten, organic silver elements and her use of form and structure are central to her design thinking. The earrings shown here were a bridal commission.

Construction Considerations

When manipulating the square wire structure into the required shape it is checked against the sketch book designs for accuracy.

Maria bends the wire into the basic shape using half-round pliers. These enable her to create curves using the rounded end of the pliers on the inside of the shape without putting any marks or nicks into the silver surface. The ends are now soldered.

Maria now lightly hammers the wire frame on a steel stake. She will retain the hammered texture this creates as a decorative feature. **Note:** for a smooth, highly polished finish use a hide mallet instead.

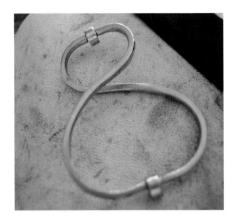

Jump rings are soldered to the upper and lower parts of the wire structure to accommodate the bezel settings. The silver is now cleaned with emery paper.

When making a setting for an unusual shape of stone it is a good idea to make models in slightly different sizes in a cheaper metal, as done here in brass. Each setting is coded and the length of the metal strip recorded for the true setting in silver.

A thin strip of silver sheet is soldered inside the setting to 'back' the stone, This has the dual benefit of raising the stone in the setting and allowing light to pass through it.

A quick way to make a small quantity of jump rings is to use round nose pliers and wrap round wire around these to form a short coil. This is then taken off the pliers and the links sawn apart using the piercing saw.

The ends of the jump link are filed and positioned at the top of the setting. It is held in place for soldering using spring tweezers.

The outer edge of the setting is filed at a 45° angle – this is to thin the metal wall and make the setting process easier when the metal is pushed over the stone.

The amethyst is placed in the setting and using a setting tool called a pusher, the metal is literally pushed over the edge of the stone.

Tube for the aquamarine setting is selected by placing the stone in the chenier and checking that the wall thickness is adequate.

Maria uses a burr bit in the pendant drill to remove some of the tube wall thickness in the upper part of the tubing, this will allow the tube to be more easily manipulated.

A chenier cutter is used to hold the tube level for sawing to the correct length, and then to file both cut edges flat, as seen here.

Maria anneals the metal to soften it and to prevent it splitting. The chenier is now stretched and opened-up further by placing it in a chenier plate and gently tapping the upper area with a doming punch.

The fluted tube settings.

A slot is filed into the bottom of the setting using a square needle file. A strip of metal is then soldered into this slot to accommodate the ear post.

Half-round jump links are soldered and the upper, outer part of the tube is filed in preparation for setting.

The ear post is soldered and finally the acquamarines are set. **Note:** prior to setting ALL finishing must be done. The stone setting is the final process.

The finished earrings showing both front and reverse.
Note: always bear in mind that the wearer sees the front of the earring when looking at their reflection, but everyone else sees the back and side. Remember this when designing.

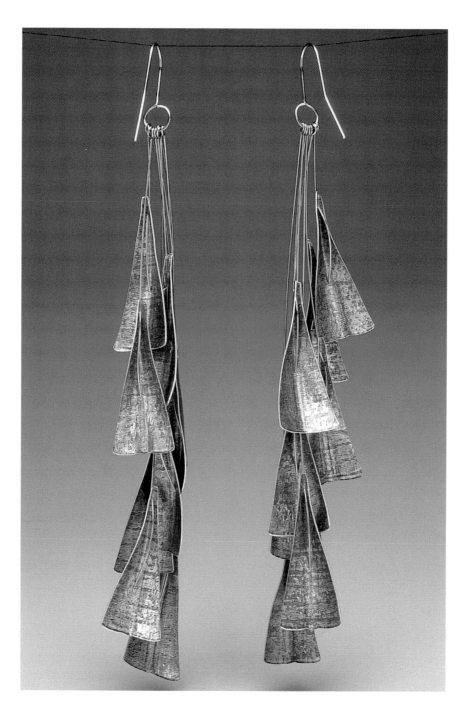

Above: Jane Adam, *Hanging Earrings*, anodised, dyed and crazed aluminium and stainless steel, 2002. Photograph by Joël Degen.

4
Metals and materials

Developing designs and ideas inspired by the material(s) used is a very personal process, as it often involves considering alternative methods of working and/or adapting traditional jewellery skills. Study can begin during training and continue to be a lifelong interest, or even an obsession. The jewellers in this chapter have all developed processes and pushed their medium to its limits and beyond.

During her MA at the Royal College of Art, **JANE ADAM** carried out hundreds of tests and experiments on aluminium. This gave her the knowledge, experience, enthusiasm and confidence to set up her workshop and earn her living from making jewellery. Aluminium is the primary material that she works with, apart from fittings that are either stainless steel or 9-carat yellow gold, used for colour and strength. Adam has explored and researched this metal for over twenty years, painting it with bold marks and pattern, carving it from thick blocks to create form and dimension, reticulating it and making it craze and crack. A recent piece, shown in opposite, is a composition of simple shapes, each curved slightly to give form, enabling the printed pattern and metallic surface to move and catch the light. Hung from the ear wire at varying lengths, these shapes form a long, sensuous, elegant pair of earrings. This lightweight metal plays a significant factor in enabling Adam to produce large designs that are easy to wear.

Colour is very important to Adam. There are no restrictions in terms of application; she can apply it directly onto the surface of the aluminium, once it has been anodised, by passing an electrical current through the metal to create a porous layer into which colour is absorbed. Adam's strong interest in textiles, paper and pattern is demonstrated in her use of aluminium, as she uses the fact that the metal has form and can be shaped and textured as well as coloured.

Adam is interested in the relationship between jewellery, the wearer and the onlooker. Her work gives an alternative to the elitist message of traditional 'precious' jewellery materials. The earrings shown in

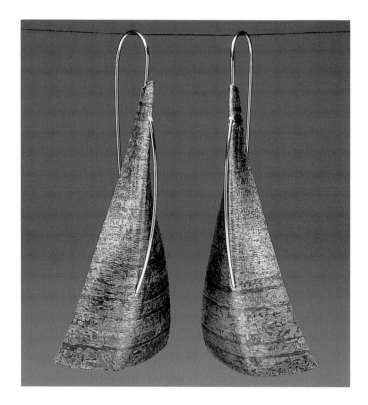

Left: Jane Adam, *Hanging Earrings*, anodised, dyed and crazed aluminium and stainless steel, 2002. Photograph by Joël Degen.

the image above have a gentler feel, both in terms of colour and pattern. Adam uses softer, simpler patterning, and there is a sophistication about this rather flattering jewellery. As always with her earrings, Adam pays attention to detail, raising the status of the ear wire by incorporating it into the design of the earring itself, turning a cheap material into something precious.

The catalyst, or starting point, for many jewellers has to be the excitement and discovery of a new material, learning how best to work with it, and then challenging it, themselves and their customer base. **KATIE CLARKE**'s interest in feathers was captured while watching fly-tying in her local fishing tackle shop. She was so intrigued by the process that she attended classes to acquire the necessary specialist skills. Clarke purposely keeps her making methods uncomplicated, choosing basic jewellery-making processes, simple fittings and findings that do not detract from the central feather features – she likes her jewellery to perform! Opposite is a fabulous example of Clarke's earrings – simplicity with drama! She begins with three pieces of silver tubing soldered together, with ear wire attached to the rear. Varying lengths of snake chain are soldered to this stud, and their ends are capped with more tubing, to hold the feathers. Thus Clarke achieves a composition of striking colours, shown off against the luxury of precious metal fittings. The chain gives movement and is a perfect connection solution between fitting and feather.

Clarke's aim is to display the feather to full advantage with an economy of process that allows her to price her work competitively. She never plans what she is going to make; for the most part, her work is instinctive and transforms her ideas into materials. She has an excellent knowledge of how ideas will work, as well as their limitations.

Left: Katie Clarke, *Mixed Reds*, sterling silver and feathers, L 10.5 cm, 2002. Photograph by Sophie Broadbridge.

Above: Katie Clarke, *Feather and Elastic Earrings and Rings,* sterling silver, feather and elastic, dia. 2 cm to 5 cm, 1996. Photograph by Katie Clarke.

Although Clarke sees her work in terms of batch production, from sleek and sophisticated to fun and furry, as shown above, she points out that because the feathers are a natural product, they are never exactly the same. She needs to match and 'pair-up' the feathers for earrings in terms of symmetry, colour and blemishes, etc. Her customer profile is vast, ageing from 12 to 86, because her range offers so much diversity in terms of choice and price. This is her strength, this ability to reach out to such a wide clientele with a product that can say different things to every individual.

Chicago-based artist **KIFF SLEMMONS** sells her work mainly to collectors, through solo or international group exhibitions, which are the primary venues for her work. She works towards these events, creating jewellery that relates to the current theme or subject of interest to her.

Slemmons's work plays with how we view objects; what happens if a familiar item is taken out of context and rearranged. Slemmons is motivated and guided by a wide array of materials, machine and clock parts, pencils, rulers, buttons and vintage portraits. She has the ability of

Above: Kiff Slemmons, *Found Rounds*, sterling silver and shell buttons, 2004.
Photograph by Rod Slemmons.

an alchemist, transforming these ordinary items into treasures, creating jewellery to be cherished and wondered at. Buttons, those precious little pieces of memory, made of mother of pearl, plastic, wood, and metal are collected, saved, and hoarded by us in all manner of ways, in boxes, bags and drawers. In *Found Rounds* (above), Slemmons treats her buttons like jewels, presenting them to best advantage. The earring pictured on the left has a slow, curving arc of six buttons, leading the eye upwards to the topmost button that attaches to the ear. The earring on the right shows an optional wear arrangement: the buttons spill out from one point, offering drama, and the black, oxidised metal arms have a zigzag profile that contrasts well with the white tips. Slemmons invites us to wear these buttons again, but as jewellery rather than to fasten our garments. By playing, organising them into different arrangements, we are harking back to the button box games of childhood past.

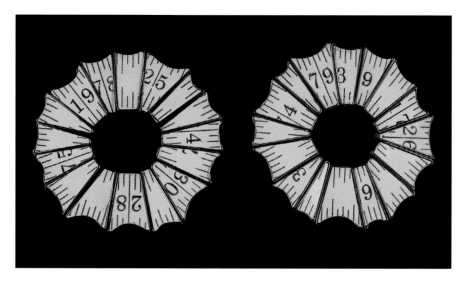

Above: Kiff Slemmons, *Found Rounds*, sterling silver and wood, 2003. Photograph by Rod Slemmons.

In the piece shown above, Slemmons takes the humble ruler and elevates it to the status of gemstone. She sets it in a frame structure of silver bezels, with the numbers and divisions creating abstract patterns against the regular yellow coating. Recognizable and yet intriguing at the same time, what exactly is being measured here and is the composition of the numerals significant?

This work is skilfully executed, both in terms of technical prowess and the strange yet familiar combinations of objects and materials that are used. Slemmons jogs our perceptions by re-ordering them and giving them a voice.

BARBARA CHRISTIE does not sell her jewellery through galleries or retail outlets; instead, she prefers to take part in craft fairs such as *Goldsmiths' Fair*, *Origin* and *Art in Action*. Christie wants to meet her customers to find out what it is about her work that attracts them to it, and in this way she has built up a strong, loyal customer base. As a teacher of part of the BA course at Central Saint Martins College of Art and Design, and Head of the Jewellery Department at Morley College London, this suits her very well, allowing her to earn her living from teaching and making jewellery, the two things that she likes best.

Christie uses her wonderful box of precious and semi-precious stones as the starting point when designing her earrings, playing around with ideas and composition options. These beautiful stones, obtained from dealers in the UK and at specialist fairs in Germany, are central to her jewellery, chosen for their colours, unusual shapes and cuts. The earrings in Fig. 28 (below) are dominated by the fabulous central baguette-shaped kyonite stones, the design's starting point for Christie. These are presented between smooth, rather striking pieces of ciment fondue with coloured inclusions, which she has shaped a little by grinding and filing. 18-carat yellow gold is used for the settings and little hinges that connect to the lower part, giving a swinging movement. Above the stone a little dot of gold separates the lower, heavier area from the upper. This device gives breathing space to the overall design, allowing it to sit easily on the ear.

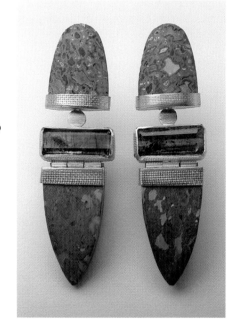

Christie's earrings measure between 50 mm and 70 mm in length, demanding attention due to their sheer size and the array of stone combinations that she puts together.

Right: Barbara Christie, *Drop Earrings*, 18-carat yellow gold, kyonite and ciment fondue with coloured inclusions, 2003. Photograph by Joël Degen.

Left: Barbara
Christie, *Drop
Earrings*, sterling
silver, 18-carat gold
settings, frosted
crystal discs,
brown diamonds,
cabochon fire
opals and matt
crystal drops,
2003.
Photograph by Joël
Degen.

The earrings shown above are a wonderful combination of luxury and
understatement, a sophisticated grouping of white, brown, orange and
18-carat gold settings.

Frosted crystal discs, with centrally placed little brown diamonds, link
to round cabochon, vibrant fire opals. These in turn connect to long,
slender, matt crystal drops. This is what Christie does best – mixing the
unusual to give a very desirable, unique pair of earrings, this jewellery is
a mixture of respect and love of material with a very shrewd eye for
composition and proportion.

KATHIE MURPHY has worked with resin for over ten years, and during this period she has refined her earring forms and colour palette to combine opaque with transparent, embedding the transparent with polyester threads. Murphy has always enjoyed working with raw materials, cooking, sewing, and the whole process of the thing. It comes as no surprise that the actual manufacture of the resin itself, the taking of a liquid and making it into a solid material via chemical process, inspires her. She produces one-of-a-kind and batch production jewellery. Though the same colour is mixed for each batch, it is never really exactly the same; because it is done by hand, it is affected by changes in temperature and even the mood of the person doing the mixing. The earrings below show off a simplicity of shape, enhanced by the unusual mix of spearmint opaque and transparent, grass green polyester threads,

Right: Kathie Murphy, *Long Earrings*, polyester resin and threads and sterling silver, L 6 cm, 2003. Photograph by Kathie Murphy.

Above: Kathie Murphy, *Stud Earrings,* polyester resin and threads, L 4.5 cm, 2001.
Photograph by Kathie Murphy.

conveying movement though the material is fixed. While the mould and
the basic form remain the same, Murphy will adjust colour and
proportion as required, thus completely altering the look of a pair of
earrings.

When worn, these earrings come alive. They are light in terms of
weight, and Murphy exploits this to good effect. The earrings shown
above consist of an upper, pale blue opaque ring and lower rectangle of
transparent resin, embedded with greenish gold threads. The pale and
transparent resins are cast to each other, and are therefore one unit.
Murphy's knowledge of her material makes this pair of earrings light
and very wearable. The opaque part conceals the ear post, and the lower
part allows light to pass through, catching the polyester threads and
creating interest. By keeping her techniques and processes simple,
Murphy can spend her creative energies on doing what she does best:
exploring and making wonderful objects in resin that can be worn on
ears and bodies.

Above: Scilla Speet, *Wing Earring*, saw-pierced units, composed and constructed using new germanium alloyed silver developed by Peter Johns, 1997. Photograph by Graham Murrell.

There are many metal alternatives to the ones we are familiar with, such as yellow, red and white golds and fine, Britannia and sterling silver. These other metals are used for different reasons: blue, black, green and purple golds are used for their colour; refractory metals such as titanium are used for strength, despite being lightweight; and tantalum and niobium are used for their propensity to be anodised across the colour spectrum. Processes too have moved on; several decades ago industrial electroforming was being researched and used by studio jewellers. Today it is laser welding that offers alternative technical possibilities.

SCILLA SPEET's work is about investigation into new metals and processes. She is known for her willingness to experiment and enter into collaborative work with other experts in different fields with access to new materials and techniques. Speet views this as an opportunity to build a rapport with fellow knowledgeable experts and to share ideas.

The earring shown above came about as a way of testing solders with germanium silver, a recently developed alloy that is firestain and tarnish resistant. This work is about quality production – one-off earrings that can be produced in quantity. *Wing Earring* is made up of several pierced units composed and constructed in this new alloy, which was developed by Peter Johns. The discovery that this metal could be spot-welded was a major breakthrough, as silver normally rejects the weld. Another benefit is the fact that it is non-allergic.

Speet sees her role as a designer at the forefront of research at Central Saint Martins College of Art & Design, where she is Course Director of Jewellery. It is important that her work gets published, so with this in mind she takes part in exhibitions, competitions and is featured in magazines. Speet uses the knowledge gained from those at the forefront of research in their particular fields, to go beyond conventional methods of designing around what is possible. She must also be practical, as her teaching commitments mean that she is only able to work for short periods of time on units, as seen in *Wing Earring.*

Left: Scilla Speet, *Aluminium Leaf Earring*, aluminium and silver wire, constructed using PVD – the physical vapour deposition of aluminium on a non-woven fabric, 2002. Photograph by Don Baxendale.

The *Aluminium Leaf Earrings* (previous page) came about out of a collaboration between Speet and **FRANCES GEESIN**, Senior Research Fellow at London College of Fashion and Central Saint Martins College of Art & Design. Geesin's work with industrial smart materials and fabrics and Speet's technical skills and approach combined to produce jewellery using a process of metallizing fabrics. The earrings are constructed using a process called PVD – the physical vapour disposition of aluminium on a nonwoven fabric. The wires running down the centre of the earrings are argentium, another alloy developed by Peter Johns, used to provide extra spring and hardness, a perfect example of using material to inform and give reason and rhythm to a design.

Sometimes a fixation can fuel a jewellers' work, for **MADELEINE FURNESS**, this fascination is lightning, being struck, scared or branded by this force of nature – the metal jewellery worn by a strike victim will leave a mark, or a 'brand', on their skin. This jewellery is concerned with paranoia and superstition. The fact that she chooses to call it 'safe' only

 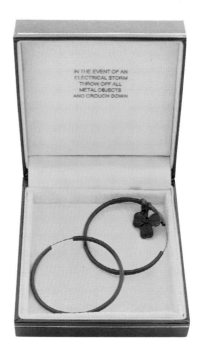

Above: Madeleine Furness, *'Lightning Safe' Jewellery - 'Lucky for Some' Scissor, and Clover*, sterling silver and synthetic rubber, 2003. Photograph by Robin Turner.

highlights and emphasizes a previously unconsidered danger. By 'mapping' the body, creating a picture via the objects it is in contact with, she makes the viewer hyper-aware of their body through the act of wearing these objects.

Furness takes a selection of metal objects in constant daily use – hairclips, metal fastenings, jewellery, belt buckles, shoes etc. – and she solders these together to create the earring (see image on p.57). Here, she uses a three-leaf clover and a little pair of scissors. She then protects these entire forms, painting them with a commercial synthetic rubber tool coating, in a bid to make the metal earrings safe from a lightning strike.

These production pieces are made from manipulated, commercially manufactured jewellery. Furness takes the traditional notion of jewellery as protection against evil and harm, and subverts this by placing it into a context where it endangers, for example by selecting the three-leaf clover as opposed to the 'lucky' four-leaf variety.

Furness questions this obsessive-compulsive activity to sanitise and make these items safe. She increasingly uses gold and silver as these are more conductive than copper, thus throwing herself and her clientele into more potential danger! Her inspiration behind these objects ranges from the safety of good luck charms to those things most likely to be struck by lightning, such as church towers and golf clubs.

The other aspect of this use of precious metals, such as 18-carat gold, 9-carat gold and silver, involves trust on the part of the purchaser as to what is underneath the black coating, though with constant wear the metal beneath will be revealed.

GRAINNE MORTON's method of gathering new materials and ideas is to be constantly on the lookout for new things, more of the same, or deviations of a current theme – anything that will catch her eye from an article in a magazine, a trip or city break, or a shopping spree.

Morton collects anything and everything, providing that it meets one important criterion – it must be small, or miniature. The one-of-a-kind pair of Charm Earrings shown opposite uses an eclectic mixture of little chickens, roses, buttons, counters, laminated butterflies, oxidised silver chain and wire. Morton tries not to sit down and design, preferring to work from a starting point, and physically making rather than doing detailed design drawings. She uses metal as a means to 'present' the contents and allow wearability by the addition of ear wires. These charm

Above: Grainne Morton, *Charm Earrings*, sterling silver and various found objects, 2004.
Photograph by Michael Taylor.

earrings allow her to use larger elements, liberating her from the boundaries imposed by working in miniature.

Morton gleans her materials from a wide variety of sources, including specialist antique shops and fairs, and dealers who will look out for particular items that are currently of interest to her. If anything, her workload is governed by the constant search for items; without them, she could not make her jewellery. The image overleaf gives a modest indication

Above: Grainne Morton, *Butterfly and Flower Ear Studs*, sterling silver, pressed flowers and paper butterflies, 2004. Photograph by Michael Taylor.

of the range of Morton's production earrings. These include laminated pressed natural flowers, butterflies and wallpaper flowers, allowing for scope and variety of materials and colour. She uses traditional jewellery techniques, but merely as a means to allow her to present the contents of her piece. Her choice of exquisite, tiny objects seems almost endless. Like Katie Clarke, the choice she offers in terms of scale, design and price means that she has very wide customer appeal. Though Morton does not make a conscious effort to reflect fashion trends, she is often ahead of the current fashion theme. She puts this down to a healthy interest in her surroundings and her constant search for new ideas.

What is it about material choice that moves artists to get excited, almost passionate about exploring and using a specific one? **SARAH CRAWFORD** will even change her way of working to suit a newly discovered material. If she needs to, she will make an appropriate tool, though her work changes so frequently that it is not worth having too many pieces of equipment for specific tasks. Her jewellery is not process driven; it is all about dealing with the surface, whether big or small.

Above: Sarah Crawford, *Lobe Gardening*, acrylic, Formica®, sterling silver and magnets, 2003. Photograph by Richard Stroud.

Crawford allows herself to be dictated to by the material and its potential. For Crawford the material just has to be 'yummy'; it really depends on what holds her interest at a particular time. Currently, this is gardening. Her jewellery is always one-of-a-kind or produced in a series. *Lobe Gardening* (above) uses layers of Formica®, Perspex® and silver. The earrings are made for unpierced ears, and use magnets to allow either part to sit in front or behind the ear lobe. The choice is further broadened by the fact that they are sold as a set of six or seven for each ear, giving the wearer a very wide choice of earrings indeed.

Ear Beans (overleaf) shows clearly how she pierces patterns and drills holes in the sheets of Formica®, to allow the lower layer to be subtly revealed, sometimes emphasizing the existing patterns, or creating her own. Crawford will add silver leaf for emphasis and detail, finally using riveting as a simple method of construction, embellishing the surface with silver dots while securing the Formica® filling between a sandwich of clear Perspex®. Crawford then files and polishes away the hard

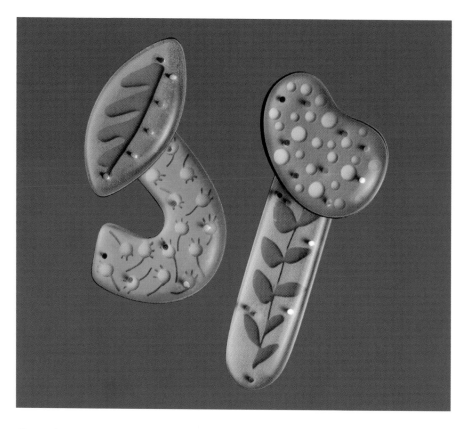

Above: Sarah Crawford, *Ear Beans*, acrylic, Formica®, sterling silver and magnets, 2003.
Photograph by Richard Stroud.

Perspex® edge, resulting in a very tactile form, not unlike a favourite
pebble or bead, but with the added bonus of also being an earring.
The drive to create something desirable out of a chosen material, to push
research and ideas to their limits, connects all of these jewellers. This, as
well as an awareness of the artist's background and thinking, turns the
casual onlooker into a fascinated observer and part of the growing
number of dedicated collectors.

5

Complex earrings

Alabaster, aquamarine and agate earrings *by Barbara Christie*
(All photographs taken by Zoe Arnold and Barbara Christie).
(See also pp. 51-52) Barbara Christie writes the following in a recent
statement about her jewellery: *'My intention is to unite a sculptural quality
with the best possible useability. It is about construction, colour, tactile
surfaces and movement. The cut of the stones I use, is decided by me and
created for me.'* Barbara Christie, Goldsmiths' Fair 2006 catalogue, p.47

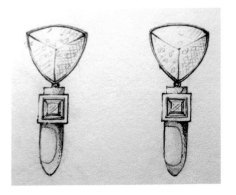

Final pencil design drawing of the
earrings to be made.

Checking the length
of metal needed for
the setting. This is
done using copper
prior to the final
18-ct yellow gold to
allow for error. The
guillotine is used to
cut the gold into
strips for the
triangular stone
setting.

The rolling mill is used to texture silver sheet. Textured paper is placed over the annealed and pickled silver, then rolled through the mills. This will be used for the outside of the back of the triangular setting.

The metal strip is cut to length and curved to follow the edge of the stone in preparation for the triangular setting. Here Barbara fits the three sides around the stone.

The setting is ready for soldering on a soldering block, the three joints have been painted with flux to prevent air getting into them. When soldering use the hottest part of the flame, to heat the centre of each side, as the metal heats it expands forcing the joints securely together. This makes for a successful solder joint.

The two triangular settings for the alabaster stones and square settings for the aquamarines have now been made and checked for an accurate fit.

The top and bottom edges of each setting are sanded flat, ready for soldering onto the silver backing sheet.

Note: no amount of solder will fill a gap. Preparation is all-important, it is tempting to 'jump' ahead but each stage must be completed before the next begun.

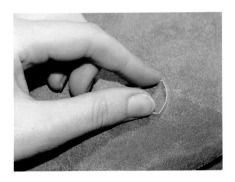

A ledge is soldered into the setting to raise the stone as it would be too thin an edge without this for the jump ring to be soldered on comfortably.

Both triangular settings are now placed on the textured silver sheet with regularly spaced pallions of silver solder. When soldering move the heat over the whole piece, concentrating it on the silver sheet as this is the largest area to be heated. It is essential that everything reaches soldering temperature at the same time.

Note: once reached, the solder will suddenly melt and flood along the joint, watching this happen is similar to watching mercury move.

The triangular setting is now pierced out of the sheet.

When piercing always hold the metal firmly and saw in a loose up and down motion, allowing the blade to move freely. This will give a more consistent cut and break fewer blades.

The tubing is cut to length for the lower setting of this earring design.

The square settings must now be filed with a half round file to enable them to fit the contour of the tube – see the black marker guide. Barbara files the contours to fit using the bench peg to support the tubing, allowing the file to move cleanly and consistently over the metal.

The lower end of the tube is ground-out using a burr bit in the pendant drill. This allows the bullet-shaped stone to fit snugly in the setting and to sit at the same distance from the edge of it.

A square hole is now made in the side of the tube, to accommodate the back of the square stone. To do this holes are drilled into the tube, ground with the burr and finally filed with appropriate needle files.

Small concave tops are now made and soldered to the top of the tube element. This will reduce the amount of connecting jump ring seen and are a neat solution to capping the setting.

First strips of silver are cut, formed and soldered into rings. These are hammered round using a ring mandrel. The little rings are soldered onto a flat piece of silver, these are then pierced out and filed flush. The 'lid' is then domed. To do this it is placed on a steel block and hammered using a doming punch to give a concave top.

The square settings are now soldered to the tube, care is taken to line these up correctly with the 'recess' holes.

Four round wire jump rings are made to connect the triangular upper with the lower tube and bullet-stone element. The edges of the settings have been filed reducing the thickness of the metal to allow for successful setting of the stones. The jump rings are first soldered to the inside of the little domed lid. The other jump ring is linked through this, closed-up and soldered to the base of the triangular setting.

Note: minimum pressure should be exerted on the stone otherwise it could crack or shatter.

Finally the earring posts are soldered to the back of the triangular element. The position, while central, is in the upper area of the setting to give balanced wearability. If truly central it would be too low and not sit well on the lobe, tipping forward uncomfortably and unattractively. **Note:** the set-up of the soldering blocks to prop-up and balance as needed.

TIP

The soldered earrings are now boiled in soda crystals to neutralise any acid inside the two elements.

The earrings are now cleaned using first needle files then emery paper.

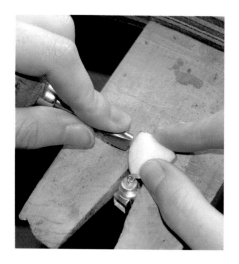

The triangular alabaster stones are set first. The bench peg is used for this, the sawn 'V' protects the earring post while also holding the earring itself securely while the metal is pushed over the stone with the pusher.

The square stones are set next. The bullet stones are now glued into the tube settings with 24hour set glue Araldite.

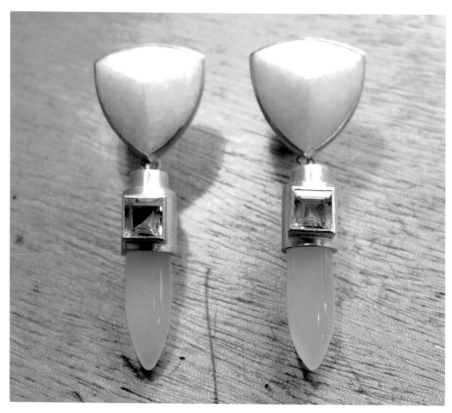

Above: The finished pair of earrings.

6

One-of-a-kind, precious metals and stones

For many people, jewellery signifies value, marking an occasion or event in one's life, with precious metals being the first choice. Names such as Cartier, De Beers and Tiffany & Co. immediately spring to mind. Other outlets include specialist shops and galleries, and studio jewellers working in very high value metals and precious stones, creating very exciting and individual pieces of jewellery.

To the enthusiast and customer, it does not really matter where they buy this jewellery. What is important is the choice of artists offered and the ambience of the outlet, making browsing or purchasing a pleasant and enriching experience. For the studio jeweller, there are vast differences in the various retail opportunities. Work can be made to order, in consultation with buyers from large department stores. Once delivered, the shop is invoiced and must pay within the time stated. Providing work on a Sale or Return basis is more likely in smaller galleries and shops.

For jewellers working in precious materials, the financial outlay can be considerable, especially if their market is a mixture of exhibition work, trade shows and selling through galleries or shops on a Sale or Return (SOR) basis. SOR work is made speculatively, in conjunction with feedback from gallery staff as to customer and collector preferences, as well as using the jeweller's own experience and dealings with clients, and knowledge gained from taking part in craft and trade fairs, and talking to others in the field. It is crucial that the work is rotated round the retail circuit, usually starting in the main London galleries, which attract all of the major international collectors and visitor enthusiasts. After several months, any unsold pieces are usually returned and a new collection is put together. Handled properly, SOR works well; the artist remains in control of his or her stock, and if it does not sell the artist can adjust the contents of the collection so that it does sell, or he or she can move items to another venue.

Above: Malcolm Betts, *Hoop Earrings*, platinum and natural coloured diamonds, 2003/04. Photograph by Lydia Lemprière.

A certain mindset, a belief in one's self and work, and consistent success at various levels of the retailing sector cultivates an opportunity in terms of reaching a wider clientele – opening one's own establishment. In 2001, **MALCOLM BETTS** opened his exclusive shop in London's Notting Hill to sell and promote his jewellery. He employs a manager to run the shop and liaise with clients. Two assistants work with him in the basement workshop. This is a perfect arrangement, as this allows him to deal with clients in the shop as necessary to discuss special requirements.

Betts's rings, necklaces, bracelets and earrings mix the best of classic with contemporary design to create work that has a subtle beauty, born out of an admiration for the metals and stones he uses. His jewellery in platinum, 22-carat and 18-carat yellow gold incorporates diamonds, sapphires, rubies, emeralds and antique pearls with flair and confidence. For the earrings shown above, Betts uses brilliant cut, natural coloured diamonds, set in individual, cone-shaped platinum settings, welded

Above: Malcolm Betts, *Drop Earrings*, platinum with antique excavated pearls, rose cut and briolette cut diamonds, 2003/04. Photograph by Lydia Lemprière.

together to form an arc. The ear post is positioned at the top of the uppermost setting, positioning a rich yellow diamond next to the lobe as the subsequent diamonds curve down and around the bottom of the ear. These earrings are complimented by the bangle, their yellow, cognac and rose-coloured stones set off by the platinum.

Betts selects stones for their colour and shape, sourcing a variety of 'old' cuts from dealers and specialist fairs that today's stone cutters are no longer trained to do. Betts chooses precious metals because he prefers to work with them over any other metal. This is born out of previous experience over a number of years, experimenting with a wide range of metals, techniques and scales, first at Middlesex University and then at the Royal College of Art, London. Precious metals give him what he needs in terms of workability, client satisfaction and investment potential, plus the longevity of his jewellery.

Betts tends to allow the stones to lead him. A perfect stone is not necessarily desirable; one with many inclusions in it can be amazing, its flaws making it sparkle and come to life. The earrings shown above use rose cut diamonds in a platinum setting. A simple sequence of jump rings connects the antique pearl and exquisite briolette cut diamonds, making an unusual, confident and rather beautiful combination of colours and extremes.

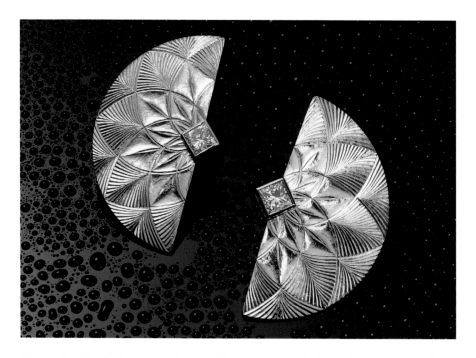

Above: Alan Craxford, *Sun Moon Earrings*, 18-carat yellow and white golds, hand engraved with yellow and white Princess cut diamonds, 0.53 carats, each 40 × 20 mm, 1997. Photograph courtesy of De Beers. Photograph by Paul Hartley.

ALAN CRAXFORD, like Malcolm Betts, chooses precious stones and metals for the sheer enjoyment of working with these materials. Craxford's feelings extend further still to issues of tradition and longevity; some of the oldest objects we know are jewellery, and jewellery made in precious metals will be around for 1000 years or more.

There is a sense of the divine in Craxford's jewellery. It is very much about the unseen world, the ancient world of gods, and again it connects to tradition and history. This jewellery incorporates complementary opposites, yin and yang, dark and light, night and day, and symbols such as the sea, sky, sun, moon and stars. The mandala, and the many ways it is depicted in both Buddhist and Hindu religions, is for Craxford a source of wonder and spiritual exploration; with its many-layered meanings, the circle is a shape that appears again and again in his jewellery in a variety of guises.

The earrings shown above are handsome and large in size, giving a sense of weight and presence. Craxford uses traditional hand engraving and carving to achieve depth and movement in these wonderful, intricate earrings. The materials further enhance the subject of opposites, the sun and moon. The 18-carat white and yellow golds are each set with a yellow and white Princess cut diamond. These diamonds are given alternate gold settings, which presents a composition that focuses the eye, compelling the viewer to wonder at the meticulous craftsmanship of the engraved pattern.

Craxford never does specific illustrative drawings; rather, he draws to capture the spirit as opposed to the finished piece. Colour too plays an important role in Craxford's jewellery. Platinum, niobium, coloured golds, enamel, coloured diamonds and tourmalines, for their wide colour spectrum, are used to achieve the effect he seeks. In the work shown below, tanzanites were chosen for their captivating purple-blue colour, a perfect companion for the 18-carat green gold. Here Craxford engraves a delicate feather design onto the gold in such a way that the engraved lines shimmer with light as it crosses the surface of the metal. The

Left: Alan Craxford, *Feather Drop Earrings*, 18-carat green gold, hand engraved with trillion cut tanzanites, 40 mm drop, 1999. Photograph by Joël Degen.

triangular shaped tanzanites – tips facing upwards – complement the gold feather form, which faces downwards, giving a simple area of space between the upper and lower parts that allows the feather to move freely when worn. Craxford's work is changing and developing all of the time, with each unique piece exploring the inner world for both himself and his clients. Thus he adds a little to the 7000-year tradition of making jewellery.

Above: Daphne Krinos, *Earrings*, oval aquamarine cabochons set in 18-carat yellow gold, with three hexagonal aquamarine crystals, 2004. Photograph by Joël Degen.

The theme of Greekness present in **DAPHNE KRINOS'S** jewellery has much to do with her being born and having lived half of her life there. She uses 18-carat yellow and green gold (an alloy with no copper), and makes no attempt to hide her hammer marks; rather, she wants to show how the piece has evolved. Translucent stones and oddly shaped crystal beads are also used. It is important to her to have light passing through, like the 'sea washed' glass she collected as a child.

This is seen in her earrings when worn, as when hanging from the ear, light is able to pass through this cluster of unusual beads. The earrings shown above comprise of oval aquamarine cabochons set in

18-carat yellow gold. The setting has the luxury of a frame with a decorative wire edge, and connects to three hexagonal aquamarine crystals. Krinos has fabricated little 'capped' ends for the beads in 18-carat yellow gold, rather than threading the predrilled core to attach these in a more conventional manner. She sets herself these 'tasks', forcing herself to discover new solutions, consider alternative features and push her ideas further, breaking free from the traditional mindset and rigours of jewellery making.

Krinos does not draw her designs beforehand, preferring to work directly in the metal. It is all about the feel of the material that she is working with, and the processes she is using. Semi-precious stones such as tourmaline, aquamarine, citrine, amethyst and iolite are favourite choices, bought for their interest value rather than investment. She would rather not use a stone than compromise over sub-standard form or colour. The earrings shown below comprise of 18-carat gold with round

Left: Daphne Krinos, *Earrings*, 18-carat yellow gold with round and oval cabochon tourmalines, 2004. Photograph by Joël Degen.

and oval cabochon tourmalines. Here Krinos cuts thin, hammered strips of metal to attach the lower, smaller cabochon to the upper part. Several curving, round gold wires are added to complete the piece. This is typical of the sensitive nature of her jewellery, as she works intuitively to create a part that looks correct in relation to the piece as a whole.

Krinos enjoys working to a brief. She might choose an oddly-shaped stone or bead, or a slice of stone, and ask 'How do I deal with this?' In this way she is able to give herself a sense of freedom, which allows her to be spontaneous, to make work that is exuberant and interesting, and is typical of the maker herself as well as her jewellery.

For jewellers working with precious materials, working to commission is often a vital part of their business. For many clients, being able to meet and talk to the artist, select stones, choose metals, and to be involved with the creation of a special piece of jewellery is a very exciting and worthwhile experience. A client might choose a jeweller because of a piece he or she has seen that was not quite right for one reason or another, or it may be that the artist's design style and choice of metals and materials is in keeping with the client's desires. It might also be that, due to a previous commission being such an enjoyable and worthwhile experience, this is now a preferred way of purchasing special items of jewellery for the client.

CATHERINE MANNHEIM enjoys the commissioning process. Her customers range in age, gender and profession, and recently she has been approached by a lot of younger clients who are looking for individuality and to express something of themselves in what they wear. Mannheim's inspirations are the metals that she chooses to work with and the stones she uses. She treats her materials like a picture, using colour and texture in a variety of ways in terms of composition and proportion. She began including stones in her jewellery fifteen years ago in response to client feedback, preferring to use them as an accent, not a focal part of her design. This restraint comes from several sources, including early ideas inspired by her mother's collection of jewellery made by a Bauhaus-trained silversmith and a year spent at the Werkkunstschule in Dusseldorf, Germany, where she studied under the formative teacher and jeweller Fredreich Becker, also working for him at weekends. Added to this is Mannheim's interest in Japanese sword making, the different

Above: Catherine Mannheim, *Earrings*, 18-carat white and yellow golds with square sapphires, 1998. Photograph by FXP.

materials and alloys that were used for this, and the flat 'floated' patterns that decorate Japanese lacquer boxes.

The earrings shown above are made of 18-carat white and yellow gold. Alternating colours and shapes, squares, rectangles and triangles are presented randomly in a circular composition. These thick chunks of precious metal form a frame around the central void. In the upper area of this space, Mannheim positions a square sapphire. The units themselves are similar but placed at different angles in each earring, and the effect is calculated, simple yet spontaneous.

This is Mannheim's strength – knowing how to create a design that has maximum effect by using uncomplicated, almost minimal means. She likes to think about her ideas, as they are a continuation of her experience; each new design evolves from previous ones, which inspire, inform and in turn lead onto another. Mannheim thinks ahead about saleability, maintaining that much of what a jeweller makes is influenced by what they know they can sell. She knows that while her customers want sophistication, they also want earrings that can be worn easily, on a variety of occasions, whether their dress is smart or casual. She provides this by mixing metals to give detailed accents of pattern laid on

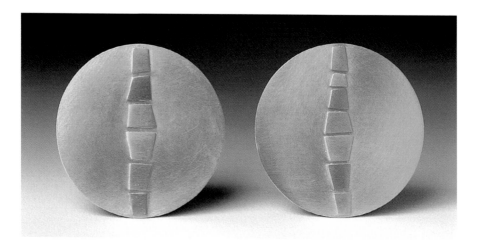

Above: Catherine Mannheim, *Earrings*, 18-carat yellow gold discs with central line decoration in 18-carat white, green and 22-carat golds, 2003. Photograph by FXP.

a simple background. In the earrings shown above, the 18-carat yellow gold discs and central line of decoration in 18-carat white, green and 22-carat golds are understated, yet they draw the viewer in to consider the sequence of the coloured golds and admire the matt finish that so enhances this almost effortless detail.

In many ways, one might think that precious metals, stones and traditional jewellery techniques would result in fairly repetitive designs. With the work of studio jewellers practicing today, this could not be further from the truth: while the materials and skills may be similar to those used for centuries, attitudes and visions have moved on and are in many cases very diverse. Skill is vital in the work featured in this chapter because of the nature and sheer financial value of the materials involved. It is fascinating how each jeweller featured has certain attributes that set him or her apart from any other jeweller.

While **MALCOLM MORRIS**'s work might appear to be fashion-orientated, there is control within this ornamentation, derived from an intensive, very technical jewellery training. During his City & Guilds training Morris specialised in diamond mounting, he then moved on to work first for Andrew Grima, then Gillian Packard, before tapping into his creative side by doing a degree at Middlesex University. It is this very inbuilt control that Morris has been trying to break free from. The work featured below is a culmination of this escape. These earrings show his enjoyment of the making process; the forging hammer marks are left, rather than erased, as he would have done previously. Working with wire, controlling form and maintaining strength has been a challenge for Morris, as it is technically difficult to do. Incredibly, there are only two solder joints in these earrings, the wires instead being twisted, bent and bound into the design. The scale is large, due to the nature of the design and construction; here, space is of equal importance as the metal.

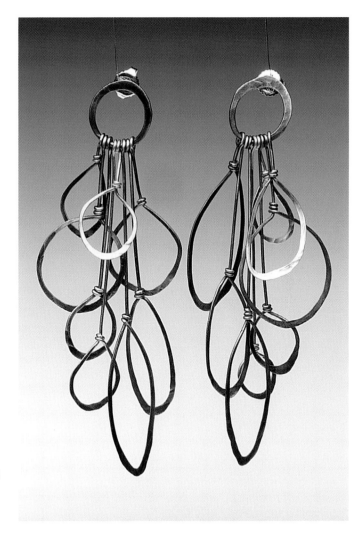

Right: Malcolm Morris, *Wire Loop Earrings*, oxidised sterling silver and 18-carat gold, L 10 cm, 2003. Photograph by Richard Stroud.

Above: Malcolm Morris, *Asymmetric Apple Blossom Earrings*, sterling silver and 18-carat gold, L 7.5 cm and 9 cm, 2004. Photograph by Richard Stroud.

The *Asymmetric Apple Blossom Earrings* are an excellent example of Morris's ability to work to commission. The customer brief was to create a pair of stunning, asymmetrical earrings in silver and 18-carat gold, inspired by Morris's *Apple Blossom* collection of tiaras and necklaces. This was a perfect opportunity for him to create an extravagant pair of earrings by mixing the ideas and techniques used in a limited-edition collection, and to push this into the realm of one-of-a-kind works, by way of client requirements. Here, Morris uses his manufacture and design skills to the full, seen in the easy handling of structure, proportion, composition and the confident use of metals and technique, along with attention to wearability. Although these earrings are long, 7.5 cm and 9 cm respectively, they are light, due to the deceptive metal thinness. They make a statement – a Morris speciality!

Scale and structure are fundamental components of **RACHELLE THIEWES'** jewellery. There are elements of performance about this work, for both viewer and wearer. It is provocative, and moves sensuously, demanding to be noticed, heard and accepted on its own terms. That Thiewes achieves all of this successfully is proof of her astute understanding of the human awareness of and need for beauty, and the desire to be individual.

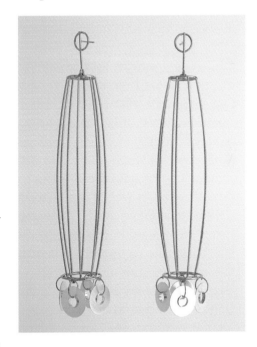

Her recent collection of earrings, (shown right), combines small, hanging, satin-finish silver discs with polished, 18-carat, palladium white gold wire configurations. The gold gives the necessary strength for these cage-like constructions, and has just the right subtle luminescence to create contrast with the silver discs. These two metals, with their satin and

Above: Rachelle Thiewes, *Shimmer Series*, 18-ct palladium white and silver, L 14cm x D 2.8cm, 2004. Photograph by Rachelle Thiewes.

Left: Rachelle Thiewes, *Shimmer Series*, 18-carat palladium white and silver, L 12.1cm x D 3.2cm, 2003. Photograph by Rachelle Thiewes.

polished finishes, combine together to flash and shimmer as light strikes them. In terms of composition, there is a sense of order, balance and poise.

As Professor of Art at the University of Texas, El Paso, Thiewes heads the metals programme. Living and working there, in this visual landscape of stark mountains and desert, the dramatic changes of light – from harsh, glaring sunlight to a soft, gentle glow – has been a strong influence on her work, thoughts and feelings. Thiewes has been interested in earrings for the past twenty years. The work shown above is an inspired example of this experience and exploration, producing sound and rhythm when worn. The little silver discs move and create noise, making the whole experience of her work exciting and unpredictable. The scale is interesting; being 12.8 cm in length, these earrings pull on the shoulders when worn thus challenging the relationship between body and jewellery, and presenting issues of structure, scale and freedom.

Despite such differences in scale and wearability, Rachelle Thiewes and Catherine Martin are both extremely aware of the relationship between earring, head and neck. Both are motivated by light, and what happens as it moves over metal.

CATHERINE MARTIN is conscious of designing for women. She sees jewellery as a part of the synthesis of fashion, textiles and garments. Martin is a practical rather than a conceptual artist; for her, jewellery is there to be worn. She does not like the idea of putting statements on other people's bodies. The customer's enjoyment from the piece is fundamental, whether the material is clay, wood or precious metal.

Martin began her career studying music, working as a professional musician before spending four years in Japan learning Kumihimo silk braiding. To acquire the necessary metal skills to further her ideas, she studied at Sir John Cass before doing an MPhil at the Royal College of Art.

A fine example of Martin's work is shown right. Within the braid is a layer of thin gold sheet, not unlike a dressmaker's pattern, dictating the long, flowing shape of the braiding. A central gold wire, like a spine, runs down its length; this raises the braid to allow light to be thrown on the two planes. When she has completed the braiding, Martin starts to manipulate it into the earring form. Great care is taken to

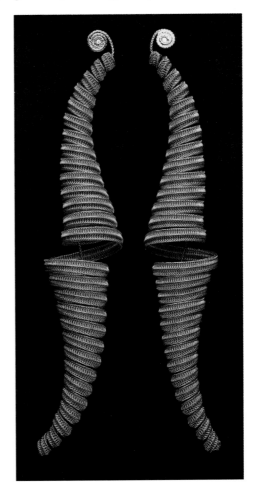

Right: Catherine Martin, *Spiral Earrings*, 18-carat yellow gold, L 7 cm, 1994. Photograph by David Cripps.

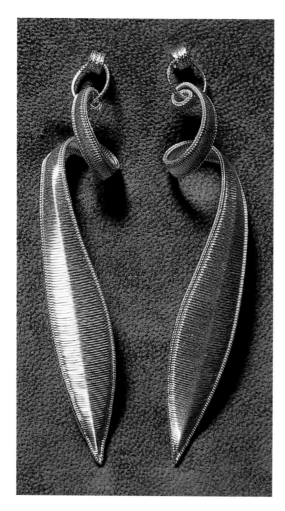

Left:, Catherine Martin, *Leaf and Coil Earrings*, 18-carat yellow gold, L 4.5 cm, 2003. Photograph by Heini Schneebeli.

avoid any damage, as the braid cannot be repaired. Here the braided form is an exuberant, curving, coiled arrangement, flaring out dramatically at the centre. This is an excellent example of Martin's ability to produce a pair of matching right and left earrings – no easy task, given that she must first work out how to bend and twist the design and then reverse her thinking to produce these spiralling earring forms that perfectly mirror each other. The top ends are curled into scrolls, to which the post is then attached. The lower ends are then curled back into this beautiful structure.

Martin works with a combination of technical prowess and a love of graceful movement, looking from old to new, wanting her jewellery to last and appear ageless in 100 years' time. In the simpler, elegant pair of earrings shown above, the post is soldered onto a coil of metal. Its hollow centre allows a ring to pass through and connect the ear post to the braided part of the earring. This allows the whole piece to turn over completely, giving an alternative choice of earring. In ancient forms of jewellery, there are many recordings of earrings enhancing the wearer's face. This is what Martin is striving for – to give enjoyment to the wearer when worn, to boost confidence and to captivate everyone around.

The vast choice of precious and semi-precious stones currently used by studio jewellers is very exciting, with colours, shapes and cuts adding to the luxurious experience of viewing and wearing a pair of earrings with a fabulous set of stones. The experts make this appear effortless, but it takes a keen eye, vision, years of experience and a love of the stones themselves to enable a magnificent piece of jewellery to emerge.

MARK NUELL has all of these talents. He is able to choose the right combination of stones and put these together, with silver and various golds, to give his clientele wonderful jewellery. His previous career as a stonecutter in Australia, and the experience derived from this, plays an important part in his work, as his knowledge of this raw material is crucial to his designing.

Above: Mark Nuell, *Earrings*, sterling silver with 22-carat gold, 18-carat gold settings, sapphires and diamonds, 2003. Photograph by FXP.

Nuell now uses a gemcutter to cut stones to his requirements. He knows what will work, and selects semi-precious stones for colour and cutting possibilities. He also incorporates faceted stones, mainly sapphires and diamonds, into his designs. The earrings displayed above show how he has transferred his stone forms into cast silver units. Here he offers his clientele choice through the variety in his designs. By using additional square, tear-drop and circular stones, he gives a range of limited edition earrings that is original, interesting and eye-catching.

Shown overleaf are some elegant silver and aquamarine drops created by Nuell. The square and oval cabochons are presented in silver units with 22-carat gold settings. This has the dual purpose of enhancing the

Left: Mark Nuell, *Earrings*, sterling silver with 22-carat gold settings, aquamarines and diamonds, 2004. Photograph by FXP.

stones' colour and, being a soft metal, gold is practical in terms of setting. A gold trefoil with three circular diamonds serves as a feature and ear stud. This confident usage of unusual shapes, the balance of metal and stone, milky aquamarine with satin silver finish, is what Nuell does so well, the simplicity belying his technical mastery.

PAUL WELLS likes to 'mess around' with bits of metal, experimenting with techniques, and moving metal about. He never measures; it is all instinctive. He uses gold and silver, as well as copper, for its malleability and colour. He does not use stones, preferring his work to be judged on its aesthetic merit.

Wells is inspired by death and decay in nature. In his jewellery he is trying to capture something, to express a little about life. The image shown opposite conveys and captures feelings of sensitivity and emotion,

Left: Paul Wells,
Pod Form Earrings,
18-carat yellow gold,
L 13 cm, 1998.
Photograph by
Paul Wells.

an appreciation of the aesthetic via these tangible, organic forms. 18-carat gold is chosen because of its workability. To cope with the techniques, he fold forms (a process of folding metal, then rolling it and hammering it to the desired shape), along with forging.

Wells is a bit of a maverick, preferring to make only what he wants to. He supports this practice by teaching at Morley College and Central Saint Martins College of Art & Design. He constantly poses questions to himself, colleagues and his contemporaries:

Is he representing what is already there?
Has it existed before, or is it original?
What makes something precious – where does the notion come from?
Is it a manmade concept, and what exactly is 'precious'?

7
Production ranges

Creating a successful production jewellery range requires a particular mindset: a measured approach to design that understands the benefits and the limitations of the manufacturing method(s) being used. With this information, the artist can then work out his or her costings, make comparisons with the relevant marketplace and plan volume accordingly.

With metal fly pressing or casting, it is crucial that the unit can have several uses, for example: a small stud as part of a larger stud with, for instance, a disc slipped behind via the post fitting; or as an ear stud with a jump ring attached that connects to lower units, giving a long, dangly earring. The range expands even more when one considers colour and finish – possibilities include natural, white or black silver, gold plate, highly polished, matt or textured finish metal. With acrylics, the designer may cast in resin or laser-cut flat sheet where the layout of the pattern is crucial to yield maximum material usage. Heat forming and dyeing will enable a still greater choice of form and colour. For a production range to be successful, it has to be appealing, offer options and be priced competitively.

In the 1980s, fellow jeweller Alison Campbell and I ran a business together, making a range of acrylic fashion jewellery. After five years, we had to concede that we were not geared up to produce in the great volume that our customer base desired. Nor were we able to reduce our prices to the competitive levels needed to increase sales and, ultimately, demand. In retrospect, we should have concentrated on one-of-a-kind or mass production, but we let the market control us. This resulted in jewellery that was categorized as production, due to pricing, when in fact it should have been presented as limited edition, with the addition of a simplified 'bread and butter' range that would have allowed us to pursue new ideas and raise our profile by taking part in exhibitions.

This chapter looks at the varying attitudes and methods used by nine very successful jewellers to create a product for a specific customer base. It pays attention to their clever and innovative usage of materials, techniques, time spent on labour and pricing to a carefully considered market.

Above: Marlene McKibbin, *Acrylic Range*, a selection of dyed and machined acrylic.
Photograph by Marlene McKibbin.

MARLENE MCKIBBIN has always been aware of the potential and the limitations of the material and area she is working in, feeding this knowledge into her jewellery ranges. McKibbin has never been interested in creating one-off work; rather, she is enthralled with the potential of repetition. In the mid-1970s, while doing an MA in Jewellery at the Royal College of Art, London, she frequented the Product Design, Printmaking and Photography departments in a bid to learn as much as she could about production in industry and related techniques. She experimented with acrylics, and investigated screen-printing, vacuum forming and injection moulding. Gradually, she began to adopt the work ethic she continues to use today, working around what is possible and readily available. Her initial batches of jewellery used precast acrylic rod, into which she drilled holes in a series of patterns. She also incorporated silk threads into the holes, machined away the surface, then dyed and heat-formed the material into bangles, resulting in an optical illusion of colour and distortion.

While McKibbin's work does not use traditional jewellery techniques, she is quick to acknowledge that the metal skills acquired in her jewellery training are essential in the design and creation of her work. Her jewellery divides into two ranges: dyed acrylic and stainless steel. The core of each is a concept that is easily adapted to allow for expansion and change as necessary. This enables McKibbin to meet customer demands, yet stay in control of what she wants to supply.

Her acrylic range is about colour. McKibbin limits herself to two colours per season or collection, allowing her to easily manipulate the 'look' of her entire range to meet demand, and by dip-dyeing the Perspex® she can offer yet more alternatives, depending on which colour is uppermost. The three earring designs, bracelet and ring shown on p.91 are simple, familiar shapes. A rich brown, yellow and a blue are used. In the half-disc earrings (top centre of image), the colours merge in a most interesting manner. The sliced, or angled, discs earrings have a central silver spot, and the post is soldered to the 'spot', passing through a central drilled hole to allow for wearability, detail and interest. The hanging rods are a 'classic' that McKibbin has been producing for over a decade. Simple and effective, they are faceted at the top, allowing the ear hook to pass through, which solves a manufacturing problem and provides interest.

McKibbin's stainless steel range, shown opposite, also develops and pushes ideas and material(s). Here, the tubing is curved and connected via a length of stainless steel wire, the ends of which evolve into ear hooks and catch. The result is subtle yet sophisticated. These five earrings, necklace and bracelet demonstrate McKibbin's ability to change a design very slightly, giving an almost totally new effect, while also expanding on ideas to offer a comprehensive collection. McKibbin has a masterly command of proportion and works with a rhythm that is now instinctive.

ANNE FINLAY also works with nonprecious materials. Her current work uses neutral tones and touches of colour, and incorporates acrylic, stainless steel, PVC and nylon. Finlay enjoys experimenting to get a feel for colour and texture before going on to consider construction and the visual appeal of a design, then adding details and decoration as necessary.

Finlay is particular, the piece has to look right, function well and be easy to wear. She selects acrylics, as they are lightweight, and stainless steel for its strength, as well as its easiness to work with. She never

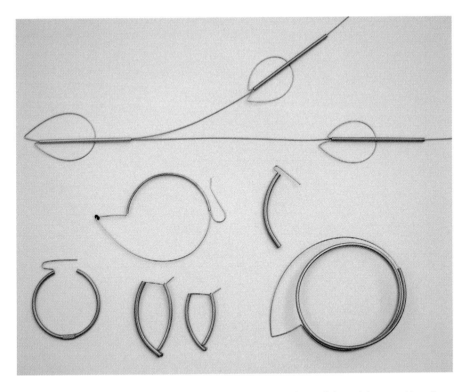

Above: Marlene McKibbin, *Stainless Steel Range*, a selection of very light stainless steel jewellery. Photograph by Marlene McKibbin.

labours too long on any one item, preferring to design swiftly and spontaneously. Her designs are geared towards production; she can cut, fold, drill and bend ten pairs of earrings in much the same time as it would take her to make a single pair. Her jewellery relies on being made in small batches to allow for competitive pricing.

When designing a new range, the brooch is always her starting point. She then considers earrings, making the fittings an integral part, or even a feature, of the design. In the image shown overleaf interest is caught by the green light-gathering rod details. In the larger earrings, this is carried through to the simple grey semicircles and fluid, curving opal rod. Balance and proportion are carefully considered, as with the simple studs, which are perfect as an accompaniment to the brooch. The brooch is itself an effective piece of body sculpture, with its green light-gathering rod enlivening the simple stainless steel tube earrings.

Finlay cuts, drills, prints and paints. She does not solder anything, but

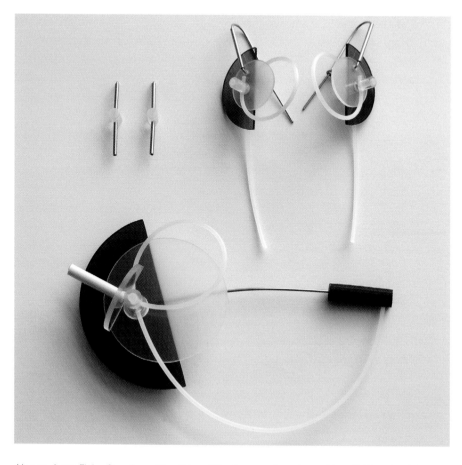

Above: Anne Finlay, *Brooch and Two Pairs of Earrings*, acrylic, nylon, rubber, PVC and stainless steel, 2002. Photograph by Anne Finlay.

instead joins the elements using wire and cable, finding ways to combine the components together that are challenging, inspiring and intuitive. The image shown opposite is an excellent example of an ear wire being crucial to the line and form of the design. Here, the wire flows down from the hook shape through the feature detail of translucent disc. On its return, it is punctuated with a length of red plastic tube. Interest is drawn back down by a second length of stainless steel wire passing through the disc and this time capped with stainless steel tube, a complex yet subtle piece of ear wear. Finlay understands her customer base and what they are prepared to pay. She designs with this in mind, using the methods she knows will give her the result she wants.

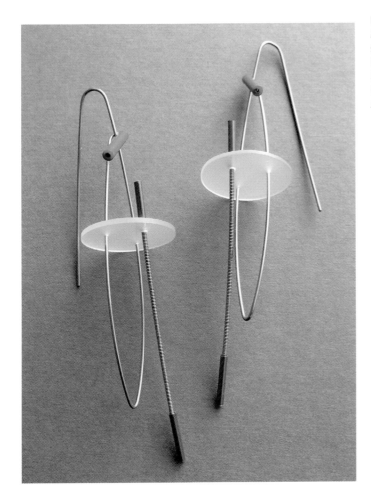

Left: Anne Finlay,
Earrings, stainless
steel, acrylic and
PVC,
L 8.5 cm, 2003.
Photograph by
Anne Finlay.

Elizabeth Bone, Noon Mitchelhill and Catherine Hills use precious metals, developing their designs to offer similar products in terms of price and range, but all have very individual approaches. Their jewellery is constructed mainly in silver, using gold plating and oxidisation to give detail and to extend the variety of the range.

ELIZABETH BONE's multi-disciplined wood, metal, ceramics and textile degree at Crewe and Alsager College taught her to play around with ideas, and explore and develop concepts. Bone always begins by making paper models of her designs. This allows her to be spontaneous and to play around with ideas, making adjustments prior to transferring the final design into metal. Like a dressmaker, Bone keeps these patterns for future reference, as they are vital in working out metal requirements, finalising construction decisions and experimenting with wearability.

Bone's circular and square range, shown below, has been in production since 1992. Its success is down to the clever balance of familiar, classic forms and shapes with a contemporary appeal. Bone began designing earrings and cufflinks, then expanded her range to include necklaces, pendants and bracelets. By using a central concave feature, she extends choice by offering black oxidisation or gold plated details.

The range uses two simple elements – circle and square – and explores almost infinite variations of circle within circle, square within circle, circle within square, and so on. This allows Bone to introduce smaller and larger units to make drop earrings, to multiply same-size units to create long, hanging earrings and to match earring to necklace to bracelet. The pieces have good weight appeal. The earrings 'feel' right when handled; they are not so light that they might evoke thoughts of 'cheap', and not so heavy that they could be unwieldy to wear.

Above: Elizabeth Bone, *Studs, Drops and Two-Part Earrings*, sterling silver with 18-carat gold plate and oxidised details, 1992-2004. Photograph by Joël Degen.

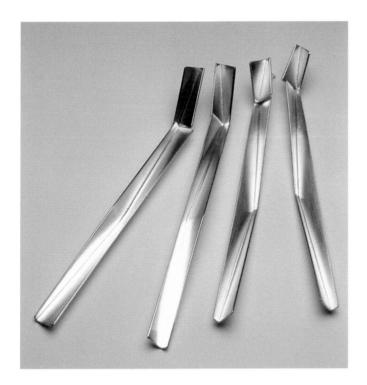

Left: Elizabeth Bone, *Long Drop Folded Earrings*, sterling silver, L 9 cm, 1998. Photograph by Joël Degen.

Bone thinks and constructs with a silversmith's, rather than a jeweller's, mentality. The way in which she considers sheet metal, and her experience and knowledge of what it will do when worked, allows her to weigh up its advantages and limitations. The work shown above is a good example of this. She uses scoring and folding to manipulate the metal in a minimal way, yet with maximum effect; the metal angles catching light to reveal form. Movement is introduced by a simple hook mechanism between upper and lower parts, to give an elegant and sophisticated pair of earrings. Having designed this range with special occasion wear in mind, Bone is astute and offers it in 18-carat gold as well as matt gold plate, offering luxury as well as a range of prices with these earrings.

For **CATHERINE HILLS**, the metal itself is really important. She aims to make jewellery that looks nice, feels right and that she knows people will want to buy. Although she enjoys making speculatively for the exhibition and gallery market, on leaving the Royal College of Art, Hills decided to be practical, to support herself and make a living from her work. The way to do this, she decided, was to create a viable range of production jewellery.

In 1995, Hills took part in the *Chelsea Craft Fair* (now *Origin*), exhibiting a small range of earrings, necklaces and bracelets. She did very well, and over the years has gradually added to her original range as well as developed new ones. It is important for her to take part in exhibitions, making one-off pieces that are often then 'pared down' into new ideas for her production ranges, a by-product that has artistic integrity and commercial viability.

Above: Catherine Hills, *Large Ear Cuffs with Detachable Snowdrop Studs*, sterling silver with 18-carat gold plate and oxidised options, dia. 3 cm cuff, stud 1 cm, 1998. Photograph by Norman Hollands.

The production range is in the main cast, with Hills making the master models in metal. She uses other techniques and equipment, such as fabrication and fly pressing, as designs require. The image opposite (p.98), shows the diversity with which she can combine and contrast metals such as gold plate, white silver and oxidised silver using a textured stud with the ear cuff. The five combinations here, in gold/black, white/gold, black/white, black/gold and white/black, are mixed as required by the customer, expanding to nine combinations in total with just these two components. Hills also offers a choice of little studs with or without the ear cuffs.

Hills's range currently offers 180 component combinations. Each design has a minimum of three and a maximum of six versions, metals and finish combinations. This vast choice allows for almost infinite display variations, meaning that Hills's work can and does sell through an extremely large number of outlets.

The work shown below is a good example of Hills's use of a cast unit and exploiting it as much as possible. Here she uses it in an earring, a

Above: Catherine Hills, *Mixed Production Range*, sterling silver and oxidised details, 1994-2004. Photograph by Norman Hollands.

bracelet, a necklace and even a ring. It can be polished/matt, white/oxidised or smooth/textured. If a design proves popular, she will produce it in a variety of sizes. These designs and the thinking behind most of her work is based on the economy of ideas, scale and ultimately the maker's time, which means that the price is affordable.

Hills is refreshingly realistic on the subject of boredom, which is unavoidable when producing such large numbers and orders. She recognises that when she is making to order, she is being paid for what she produces, as opposed to working speculatively towards an exhibition.

NOON MITCHELHILL works in silver, using gold plating and gold details to offer the customer variety and choice in her jewellery. She produces two ranges: the original, using casting as the production method; and a more recent range, using fine silver that is cut and rolled into large yet light hollow forms.

Mitchelhill is interested in pattern and surface texture. She uses gold plating and oxidation to enhance and give emphasis to this, drawing the eye in to look at little blocks of detail. Simple methods, such as lengths of wire soldered together, provide another dimension. Shown below are various alternatives she offers, with horizontal lines around a small block of vertical wires, and flat matt squares of silver contrasting with her small blocks of vertical wires with gold border details. Like both Elizabeth

Above: Noon Mitchelhill, *Production Earrings*, sterling silver and gold leaf details, 1993-2004. Photograph by Joël Degen.

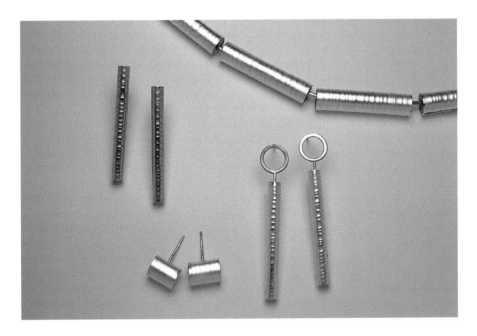

Above: Noon Mitchelhill, *Earrings and Necklace*, fine silver, 18-carat gold plate and gold leaf, 2004. Photograph by Joel Degen.

Bone and Catherine Hills, she mixes white silver with oxidised silver and gold plate to give her customer base a choice of look and price. Her combination of silver with gold plate detail is very popular, offering a price that is exactly right in terms of material and time invested in the product. Her customer, although aware that the gold is plated, is buying into a piece that says gold and silver!

When costing out her batch production work, she compares one item with others in the range, being very aware of what the market can stand and how much she can charge. She knows that she cannot exceed certain boundaries or levels, which has a major influence in her design decisions.

Time spent making and/or finishing will always play an important factor in a production item for the studio jeweller. With this in mind, Mitchelhill's recently designed range in fine silver (above) is fabricated rather than cast, offering large earrings and necklaces. She 'draws' textures onto sheets of thin, malleable metal, which is then cut and formed into earrings and necklaces. Because of the process this is production work in terms of manufacture, but limited edition due to the originality involved in the surface-drawn pattern. Mitchelhill's approach to this work is very different to that of her previous range. Rather than producing endless identical cast items, the scale of this new work has increased to better portray the delicate drawing. Wearability is not a problem, as the metal is so lightweight and needs to be a certain size to be effective. Each piece has a very individual feel and is visually intriguing.

Using a production process to inform and direct the thinking and planning of a range is another approach. **HARRIET CLAYTON** designs with three principles in mind: to produce an accessory with current fashion appeal; to use carefully planned manufacturing methods; and to charge a price that she knows her customer base will pay. Research and inspiration come from fashion designs of the 1960s. In particular, classics such as Paco Rabann's jewellery and chain metal dresses inspire her. This Clayton takes and balances with her awareness of the area she is working in and targeting.

Rather than limit herself to one material, she has recently widened her options to include silver and leather in her range of popular Perspex® designs. She addresses material wastage and concerns of weight and scale by designing a cut-out area within a necklace or bracelet, which

Above: Harriet Clayton, *Autumn/Winter 2004*, gold-plated sterling silver (a) cuff and (b) earrings. Photograph by Harriet Clayton.

Right: Harriet Clayton, *Autumn/Winter 2003, Circle and Disc Earring*, Perspex® and sterling silver, L 13 cm. Photograph by Harriet Clayton.

will then become an earring or a pendant part. The images opposite demonstrate this; here, a design for a cuff has cut-out sections that will be used as earring components.

For laser cutting to be cost-effective, the jeweller must get the maximum out of a sheet of material, whether the material is metal, acrylic or leather. Clayton does this by limiting herself to one shape. Her Autumn/Winter 2003 collection used a circle. In the image above, dangly earrings comprise of a series of discs, strung on chain. Laser-cut lines are used to give surface detail and interest, and the range of colours is dictated by fashion forecasting.

The fashion business is one that requires constant exploration of materials and methods, balanced with a desire to be original, yet offer a product that can be easily understood and worn. **SCOTT WILSON** has been working in this world for over a decade and he moves very successfully within it. During his degree at Middlesex University, Wilson did his year out placement in New York, working for Erickson Beamon. After producing a degree show collection of sculptural headwear from beads and feathers, he went on to study at the Royal College of Art, London. He did an MA in Millinery, part of the fashion department there.

Above: Scott Wilson, *Autumn/Winter 2003*, *Monetta*, leaf, silver and silver chain.
Photograph by Darren S. Feist. Makeup by William A. Casey. Model Kate Bibb @ Select.

These links between fashion and jewellery have been fundamental in shaping his work.

Wilson's business operates on two levels: the fashion production ranges that earn him his living, and fashion catwalk collections for major designers Givenchy Couture, Hussein Chalayan and Julien MacDonald, that promote the former.

Wilson's inspiration comes from rather diverse materials such as fish skin, glossy textures and seductive, metallic finishes. In terms of change and development, much is down to intuition, his love of big and bold ideas, and items with a strong graphic content and specific look. His work is not about shocking. It is more about providing jewellery that people want to buy, wear and understand. He does not want his clientele to feel threatened or intimidated.

Wilson launches a new production range twice a year, using a distinctive portrait shot of his jewellery on a model, to tie in with a particular season. There are elements of fashion trends in his jewellery, and he has consultations with a forecaster about colours, magazine features and anything that is currently relevant.

The theme of Wilson's Autumn/Winter 2003/04 collection (see image on p.104) was based on leaves, with Wilson continuing to use electroforming as the production technique. First the leaves were sealed, then sent out to be electroformed by a specialist company. The electroformed leaves returned and only needed minimal finishing before being drilled to allow fittings and long lengths of chain to be attached. Wilson's Autumn/Winter 2002/03 collection (overleaf) took feathers as its subject, using electroforming to enable the exquisite detail, ruffled appearance and soft form of each individual goose and duck plume that was replicated. These long, sensuous silver feathers were then linked to ear wires and long lengths of thin, oxidised chain by holes drilled into the quill, resulting in a simple yet magnificent earring. Each collection consists of about 60 pieces, and these divide into various groupings for the customer to select from. Wilson sells to an international market through approximately 40 stores. He has always been particularly popular in Japan, and in the UK his work can be found in a variety of outlets ranging from Harvey Nichols in London's Knightsbridge to small select boutiques such as Jess James, a couple of miles away in Soho.

Left: Scott Wilson, *Autumn/Winter 2002*, *Bird of Prey*, duck feather and silver chain. Photograph by Misha & David.
Makeup by Irene Rogers, Hair by Gow Tanaka @ Penny Rich, Model Anouchka @ FM

Today the buying pattern of a collection has changed within the commercial world. Previously, the complete 'story' was ordered, but now it depends on the store or boutique. Fashion trends and consumer spending is such that the buyer will pick and choose. Nothing has to match, and the stores and their methods of selling and display reflect this.

MICHAEL DE NARDO, like Harriet Clayton and Scott Wilson, also designs and makes jewellery with the world of fashion in mind. Having worked in this area for twenty years, for de Nardo it is the idea, and not the process, that is important. He does the designing and his designs are then made up by the team of jewellers he employs. De Nardo will try out ideas for a collection at trade shows. Afterwards, he takes customer response on board, refining, improving and expanding the range. He is a good communicator, and this enables him to make astute judgments and ultimately a range of jewellery with customer appeal.

Around 25% of De Nardo's orders are for earrings. The rest of his jewellery is mainly necklaces and bracelets. He is conscious of costs, and plans the time factor carefully. He wants to avoid prices that are cumbersome to his clientele, and with this in mind his designs therefore cannot be too complicated.

For the collection shown opposite, de Nardo responded to the recent demand for 'big' jewellery. These earrings are making a statement, offering opulence and fantasy. His starting point was a previous design, Bollywood Necklace, comprising of four strands of chain festooned with assorted brightly-coloured tourmaline and turquoise beads and discs of silver and gold. This pair of earrings is 7.6cm in length. It incorporates diamond and circle linear shapes constructed out of silver wire, adorned with an assortment of glass beads.

Above: Michael de Nardo, *Earrings*, sterling silver wire and assorted glass beads, L 7.6cm, 2004. Photograph by Kevin Nicholson.

De Nardo's designs are intended to be worn and enjoyed. He includes various familiar elements that are attractive, affordable and appealing. He regards these as the focal earrings within the range, and from this he will concentrate on certain features and simplify these, making a double circle earring with two stones, a single circle earring with two beads, a circle earring with one bead, and so on. While this may seem obvious, this is all part of de Nardo's experience and his confidence in what he does. This is borne out by his popularity with fashion buyers and their clientele.

KAZ ROBERTSON uses a surprising combination of resin, silver and magnets to create her lively and vibrant earrings. Recent colour combinations shown on p.108, in opaque baby blue with transparent cerise, and lime green festooned in pale pink dots, are challenging and confident. Robertson's intriguing use of pattern is achieved by layering up colour to obtain a very vivid vibrancy, often relating to fashion trends. By adding black and white to her colour palette, she introduces an element of sophistication to her designs, as seen here with the rather minimal yet vital use of thin cerise stripes in the left-hand earrings.

The two pairs of earrings (on the far right) have magnets inside them, allowing the wearer to put one in front and one behind the ear lobe. Robertson uses magnets to make the resin more versatile, giving alternative ways of attachment and wear.

Some of Robertson's designs are continuous. She can have ten on the go at any one time, but each is always very different in terms of feel and look. She casts her resin shapes, carving, filing and inlaying them with colour and pattern. Using rubber moulds for batch production allows her to repeat a shape an almost infinite number of times. For one-off pieces she uses cardboard moulds as this is quicker in terms of mould making as it is only used once. This way, Robertson maintains a healthy balance between one-off exhibition jewellery and batch production work.

In the image shown on p.109 interest is created by the asymmetry of this pair of earrings, and by playing with contrast and similarities. The smaller, opaque, white resin and black dot earring relates to but is not a mirror match for the larger, which although also opaque white resin, has a centre that is transparent with black dots cast into the back of this

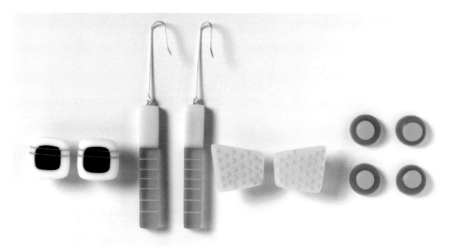

Above: Kaz Robertson, *Series of Earrings*, resin, magnets and sterling silver, 2004. Photograph by John K McGregor.

Right: Kaz Robertson, *Swinging Circles*, resin and sterling silver, L 9 cm and 5.5 cm, 2004. Photograph by John K McGregor.

area. Both resin shapes are suspended on differing lengths of chain, again creating interest and delight.

Robertson takes commercial considerations very seriously, calculating how much she must charge to realise her time and material costs accordingly. The production pieces keep her business going; she does not produce endless runs of each design, instead she controls the amounts made to allow her to progress her ideas and recognises that she would get bored doing the same thing for long periods of time. She intersperses the workload with her larger exhibition pieces, which she views as a promotional tool. Her work has a lively, honest and very individual appeal – it is easy and good fun!

Originality and variety, with a wide choice of materials and styles to suit budget and wear requirements, as well as an in-depth knowledge of manufacturing methods to better inform the design process are all key factors. This all seems rather a high list of needs, but as these nine jewellers show, it's not impossible at all. In fact, it's rather exciting.

Above: Shaun Leane, *Natural Parrot Feather Fan Earrings*. Photograph by Ben Rowe.

8

Showing off – the flamboyant and the memorable

Outrageous jewellery is created for a variety of reasons. First and foremost, it is made because the artist desires to work in this way and/or on this scale. Output has any number of outcomes. It might be working with the fashion industry, researching into new technologies, exhibition participation to convey a point of view, creating costume accessories and props for the performing arts and theatre or working in a particular way or medium because of a passion or an obsession.

As with many of the artists discussed in this book, a demanding, fine jewellery training often underpins the artist's current area of interest or business. **SHAUN LEANE** is typical of taking this route; he began his career with a five-year apprenticeship in Hatton Garden, acquiring traditional goldsmithing and diamond mounting skills before specialising in antique jewellery restoration and reproduction. This gave him a valuable opportunity to work solely in platinum and high-carat golds, and with very expensive stones, to acquire the confidence and expertise that inform and give his jewellery such poise.

Leane is responsible for the fantastic jewellery and bodywear creations that enhance designer Alexander McQueen's fashion shows. He uses any and every metal – gold, silver, aluminium or brass – whatever will give him the desired look and scale to withstand the rigours and demands of the catwalk. Stimulus from a wide variety of sources and technical virtuosity allows Leane to make whatever he sets his mind to. The work shown opposite is large enough to be seen by the audience and make a statement, while also complimenting McQueen's dress design. A silver cuff slips round the ear, and tubing is soldered onto the curving metal at intervals to accommodate around 40 colourful and vibrant parrot tail feathers, adorned with lengths of silver tube that catch light and create interest.

Left: Shaun Leane, *African Neckwires and Hoops.* Photograph by Ben Rowe.

Each catwalk piece can demand a different technique, and Leane will use whatever he needs to achieve the desired effect. He is as comfortable constructing fabricated forms in precious metals and stones as he is with using alternative materials and methods such as electroforming over a specially cast resin form, to create large structures that are light enough for McQueen's models to move easily around in.

The work shown above takes inspiration from tribal cultures, using female beauty to reinforce age-old requirements of desirability, elegance and measures of wealth shown by the number of rings worn. The series of silver plated brass hoops are all hand polished. This is lengthy and precise work, but necessary to achieve the required look that Leane and

McQueen desired. Whatever Leane creates, it is made with minute attention to detail; his previous fine jewellery training ensures a quality item.

Leane's catwalk work informs his commercial collections. His style is modern and clean cut, while also inspired, in particular by his interest in Art Deco and Victorian jewellery. His work is innovative, taking and developing aspects of his research and incorporating this into contemporary design. His silver and pink rodalite earrings (shown right), a combination of a production method and hand finishing. The metal form is a casting, with the stones all set by hand.

Above: Shaun Leane, *Silver and Rhodalite Flower Talon Earrings.* Photograph by Tim Brightmore.

This allows Leane to offer his client a fabulous pair of earrings at a viable price.

It is always fascinating to discover what inspires an artist. **ADAM PAXON** readily acknowledges that he has several influences, including Niki de Saint-Phalle's use of scale and colour, Andrew Logan's exploitation of mirror and pattern in his wild mosaics and Peter Chang's technical expertise and usage of acrylics. In his year out from Middlesex University, Paxon used his placement to learn about silicone casting, using resin and pigments while working on the sets of the films *Judge Dredd* and *Braveheart*. This was important in terms of gaining knowledge about these materials, while also giving him the confidence to increase the scale of his jewellery.

Paxon does not intend for his work to be instantly recognized as jewellery; he views his pieces more as objects in their own right, as they appear at different stages of their lifespan, currently created at their

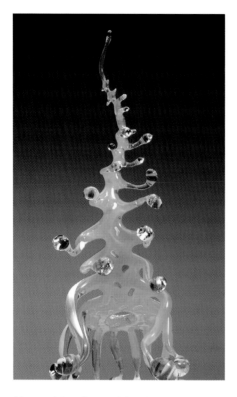

Above: Adam Paxon, *Adrenaline*, acrylic and polyester, H 28.5 cm, 2003. Photograph by Graham Lees.

reproductive peak. The work shown left, is a perfect example of Paxon's vividly coloured acrylic creatures. Although this is not an earring itself, it is important to recognize that this piece, made first, went on to inform and inspire him in the making of the Tentacle Earrings shown on p.115 (opposite, above). These have the feeling of being cut from the larger object to become little individuals, existing despite this supposed surgery. As with all of Paxon's earrings, they are designed to fit well on the ear and sit free of the head and neck, allowing light to pass through and spill out, casting coloured shadows onto the body, as shown here on the model's jaw line.

Paxon uses various types of sheet acrylic as his main material; opaque, clear, translucent, fluorescent and mirrored, he applies various lacquers to the surface interior, while stainless steel is used for the ear posts. He particularly enjoys transforming this hard-edged, commercially coloured material into a piece of jewellery that has a strange softness and allure about it. The image of *Earpins* (opposite,below) shows an intriguing selection of earrings, though it is not obvious at first how they are worn. Closer examination reveals that the fitting is enclosed in the stalk, or bulbous end, of each earpiece. This is typical of Paxon, using attractive colours, like sweets, and successfully enticing and attracting us to these little individuals.

Paxon's work has become richer, larger and more self-assured, as his ability to manipulate his material has expanded. His pieces have a character and presence whether on the body or at rest, or even placed on a surface like a little colourful sculpture – what viewer could resist being seduced by them!

Right: Adam Paxon, *Tentacle Earrings*, acrylic, various sizes, 2003. Photograph by Graham Lees.

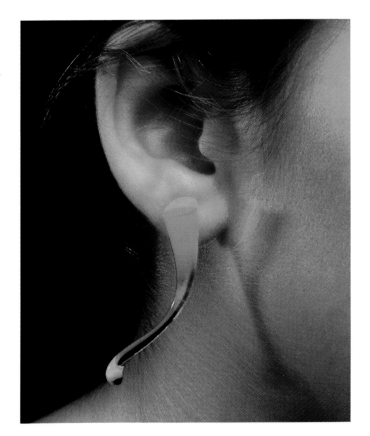

Below: Adam Paxon, *Ear-pins*, acrylic, top: L 7.5 cm, right: L 8 cm, left: 8 cm, 2003. Photograph by Graham Lees.

Left: Stanley Lechtzin and Daniella Kerner, *Auricle - MagEarrings*, glass-filled polyamide (nylon) and rare earth magnets, L 8.5 cm x W 6.3 cm x D 3.5 cm, 2004. Photograph by Stanley Lechtzin.

Exploration of material, process and available technology is an area that has significance for certain artists. The desire to discover new procedures and methods of working is of major importance to **STANLEY LECHTZIN** and **DANIELLA KERNER**, both of whom teach at Tyler School of Art in Philadelphia, USA, working together in the very specialist area of digital craft in jewellery design and production.

In the 1960s, Lechtzin was one of the first studio jewellers to experiment at length with electroforming, receiving various awards and accolades as well as research grants and exhibition opportunities in the USA and the UK. In 1978 he began researching digital technologies; the use of computer-aided design and rapid prototyping as a new working method followed. It is this area that Lechtzin and Kerner are exploring and developing, while acknowledging the importance of our traditional inheritance. A precious metal such as gold, from the past, might be incorporated into a piece made mainly in photosensitive epoxy, from the present, but used in such a way as to make it an object of the future when compared with more familiar examples of precious jewellery.

Exploring new materials and processes has always motivated Kerner. Much of her work has used a variety of plastics; her earlier jewellery favoured acrylics, whereas now, working with the rapid prototyping (RP) processes, she uses polymers such as nylon and epoxies. Kerner likes to take a material that has been developed to produce domestic commodities in large quantities and turn around pre-conceived assumptions about material usage and preciousness, using it to make special, unique pieces. She creates exciting forms in plastics with intricate detailing using Computer-Aided-Design (CAD) and Computer-Aided-Manufacture (CAM), without having any physical involvement in the manufacture process. This allows her to put all of her energies into the design conception of the next piece, which for her is a more important use of her time and skill.

The realistic rendering shown on the previous page is an interpretation of the CAD model. Lechtzin and Kerner created these earrings specifically for this book. They are computer-modelled and fabricated by Selective Laser Sintering (SLS), made from glass-filled polyamide (nylon). Each earring has two toroid rare earth magnets placed front to back. When worn, the earring is held onto the ear lobe by the strong magnetic force.

In the second image, shown below, the earrings have been RP'd and are shown being worn. Lechtzin and Kerner like to think of the CAD model as something to be interpreted by whoever manufactures the physical object.

Lechtzin and Kerner want their work to be interacted with and discussed on several levels: to be worn, for both wearer and viewer to interact with the piece; to be questioned, regarding its manufacture; and to be examined, regarding the design, while the creators' aesthetic judgements and impetus are discussed. This is a generous gesture, which only artists with strong beliefs and self-assurance in their area of expertise could offer.

Right: Stanley Lechtzin and Daniella Kerner, *Auricle - MagEarrings*, as opposite, being worn. Photograph by Stanley Lechtzin.

Left: Zoe Arnold, *We should take care not to make the intellect our God; it has, of course, powerful muscles, but no personality*, various woods, sterling silver, 18-carat yellow gold, diamonds, mirror and glass, H 23 cm, W 13 cm, 2004. Photograph by Zoe Arnold.

Many artists see their work in an exhibition context, made for audience appreciation and interaction. This often evolves from having strong views and/or a fascination with a specific subject. **ZOE ARNOLD**'s enthusiasm embraces several intriguing areas: automata, and clock movements; objects in miniature: and dollhouses, models and maquettes. She is also enthralled with issues involving the uncanny, and its portrayal by various filmmakers, including David Lynch's early film *Eraserhead*, the Czech animations of Jan Svankmeyer, and, in particular, *Alice*, and *Institute Benjamenta* by the Brothers Quay. She uses this to dream, ponder and enrich her study of the unusual. '*Zoe Arnold delights in creating unusual treasures, beautiful curios to secretly savour, which may be tailored to embrace a favoured story or personal reflection.*' Zoe Arnold, Goldsmiths' Fair 2006 catalogue, p.20.

Arnold has a unique way of developing a piece – she plans it completely in her head. Occasionally she will record it as a drawing on paper, but only for reference in case she needs to return to it or adapt the idea. The drawing on paper will be exactly the same as the one in her head.

Arnold's work shown on p.118 takes its title from a quotation by Albert Einstein: *We should take care not to make the intellect our God; it has, of course, powerful muscles, but no personality.* This is a kind of shrine. It could be a shrine of intelligence, or maybe it is for someone who is creative rather than brilliantly intelligent.

Arnold began by thinking about heads, designing and mentally carving them out of wood. The head is the central piece, pulling all of the other components together. The mirror behind the head can be moved; here, it is angled downwards, showing the back of the head; and when positioned upwards, its gaze changes to reflect the viewer's eyes. The 18-carat gold wings are not normal wings made of feathers; instead, they are leaves that are trying to reach out to somewhere. The silver cloud, pavé set with diamonds, represents dreaming and aspirations, which are almost capable of flight. This is all encased in a glass dome and mounted on a turned, painted wooden stand housing the automata workings, complete with handle.

In Arnold's piece, shown right, the earring is the fly sitting outside of the intellectual activity going on within the dome, signifying that this creature is only halfway through the thinking process. But this 'fly on the wall', made in 18-carat

Right: Zoe Arnold, *Fly Earring*, 22-carat and 18-carat golds, 1.3 cm, 2004. Photograph by Zoe Arnold.

and 22-carat golds, has status and presence, despite its small size and oneness. Arnold wants the wearer to recall the contents of the dome when wearing the little gold earring. This earring, however, is not the endearing little object it might seem. She has chosen this subject with typical wit; the fly has an unpleasant reputation, as it spreads dirt and disease – not the nicest of insects.

As the handle turns, the movements within the dome are not necessarily what one would expect. The cloud turns on its wheel and the gold wings flap, but the bottom jaw remains stationery. It is the top of the head that moves, tilting back as a simple loop of wire attached to the handle is pulled up and down. Arnold aims her work at automata collectors; these enthusiasts have a reputation for being eccentric and very secretive about themselves and their collections. Perhaps they are the perfect clientele for this unconventional jeweller.

The desire to express one's feelings and views using jewellery as vehicle or vessel is gathering momentum. By the very nature of historic association with preciousness, what better way to deliver a poignant message than by wearing it.

KEITH LEWIS uses sexual imagery as subject matter, challenging society's narrow, held beliefs towards sex – these misplaced and misunderstood assumptions, perhaps born out of ignorance and frigid fears. In 1996 he wrote the following statement contextualising his position and feelings,

> *My jewelry testifies to the ambiguity of being a queer man lost in America. It scrutinises this crabbed and bitter nation through the clouded saline lens of a diminishing community, dwindling under the onslaught of diseases of the body and of the body politic. As virus and virulence buffet us, I navigate the slipstreams of heart, gonads and conscience – making jewelry as records of lost chances, vessels of memory, quiet calls-to-arms and as talismans of grief.*

With his previous work, Lewis used a variety of techniques such as electroforming and die casting to produce hollow, sculptural torsos, their animal heads and decoration dealing with homosexual worries, sexual anxiety, emotional fragility, the awful realities of HIV and AIDS, illness and death.

Left: Keith Lewis,
Hand Earrings,
sterling silver,
diamonds and
pearls,
8 cm x 4 cm,
2004.
Photograph by
Keith Lewis.

His new body of work, created during a one-year sabbatical from Central Washington University, where Lewis is Associate Professor of Art, adopts a rather different approach. In the work shown above, Lewis incorporates fine jewellery skills such as filigree, stone setting, engraving, enamelling and casting to create rather stylised, two-dimensional forms, their contents celebrating heterosexual sex, managing to be both crude and sensitive at the same time. This work reflects Lewis's research into ancient Greek and Roman imagery, depicted on vases, frescos, mosaics and statues, for the then public gaze has been a catalyst in terms of both content and the relaxed manner in which this was visually available. The drawn enamel ovals are framed in an intricate filigree profusion of male and female genitalia, incorporating diamonds and pearls to signify semen and woman's sexual arousal. These are valuable jewels, a contemporary alternative to the classical choice of flowers and abstract pattern. The drawing is suggestive, erotically tasteful, and balances well with the richness of the filigree work.

This collection, when worn, could be seen to be taking on the role of enlightener for present-day society, depicting what was a natural part of the culture of the ancient classical world, in a contemporary manner. In the earrings above, the ornamental surface is a plethora of genitalia, with pearls being used to refer back to the preconceived values that we place on jewellery and its associations with preciousness.

In many ways, there is a humorous element amongst all of this 'shocking' jewellery. This is a vehicle with which to expose hidden feelings and offer alternative views, a door that is ajar. But who will have the courage to admit to opening it?

Some of Canadian artist **BARBARA STUTMAN**'s most formative childhood memories are of her grandmother's love of jewellery. She taught Stutman to knit and crochet and, years later, everything fell into place when she took part in a workshop taught by Mary Lee Hu, a leading practitioner in the use of textile techniques in jewellery. Using metal wire in this way was a major turning point for Stutman; she had found her medium, and could apply this to the skills she learnt as a child alongside her mother and grandmother, as part of the community of women from past, present and future.

Since 1990, Stutman has used narrative within her work, expressing herself via textile techniques to reinforce her views. Her work nudges the viewer's conscience and awareness with its refreshing honesty and 'take' on being female in today's world. Stutman deals with issues such as adolescence and sexual identity, looking at both good and bad life experiences. Her choice of knitting and crocheting to produce this work is fundamental in reinforcing the messages within this jewellery. From a historical perspective it can be viewed in two ways: the subversive stitch that kept women occupied or as a vehicle with which these women could express themselves and their lot in life.

Right: Barbara Stutman, *How to hold onto a good thing*, fine silver, copper, brass, nickel silver, cord and polyurethane pad, 12 cm x 4.7 cm, 1995. Photograph by Pierre Fauteux.

The work shown above, *How to hold onto a good thing*, was inspired by an advertisement for Chanel's 'Coco'® perfume and addresses the ways in which women are epitomized in advertisement campaigns. A beautiful, sexy woman was presented as a pet preening herself for the delight of mankind, who clasps the red leash around her ankle with a firm grip, reinforcing the legendary role of woman as man's plaything. Stutman's earrings underline this, with their slender, delicate little legs, shackled by red chain, trying to escape from overly large, manly hands. She further explains in this statement extract:

It is important to understand that representations not only reflect or reproduce the ideologies of a culture – they actively produce particular beliefs. Sexuality can actually be defined in representations: since personal identities are grounded in our place within the social, and since we continuously interact with the world, our identities, sexual and otherwise, are in constant flux and so can be affected by practices or representation.

Above: Barbara Stutman, *Maintaining the Status Quo*, fine silver, sterling silver, copper, electrical wire and jade, 8.2 cm x 5 cm, 1993. Photograph by Pierre Fauteux.

In Stutman's work *Maintaining the Status Quo*, (shown above), a pair of stiletto heels is trampled from on high by big, brash, male boots. The use of familiar feminine techniques, such as crocheting and twining, wrong-foots her viewer; what seems a delightful pair of earrings on closer inspection is, in fact, rather provocative, and it raises previously ignored issues.

In *Narrowing the Gap* (opposite) made two years later, the woman's shoe is positioned above the male's, but not in a threatening position, as it might be if the high heel were grinding into the shoe below. The feeling evoked here is conciliatory rather than confrontational, more of 'we are all in this together, let's try to make it work'. By using jewellery to educate her audience, Stutman acknowledges and confronts uncomfortable, and sometimes degrading, situations, offering future hope through awareness.

Right: Barbara
Stutman, *Narrowing
the Gap*, fine silver,
sterling silver,
copper, brass,
nickel silver and
polyurethane pad,
8.9 cm × 4.5 cm,
1995.
Photograph by
Pierre Fauteux.

ANGELA O'KELLY, like Barbara Stutman, is fascinated by the
possibilities of using textile techniques in jewellery. O'Kelly is equally
enthralled by the materials she sources to work with: paper, textiles, felt
and paper string. These she then dyes with colours influenced by her
natural surroundings. Her colour palette has progressed from native
Irish bog land browns, creams and greens, first used in her
Edinburgh College of Art degree show, to the vivid pinks, greens, oranges
and reds of seaweed in Orkney, encountered during a summer working
there for textile artists Tait and Style.

   O'Kelly is currently manipulating textile techniques. For the work
shown overleaf, she used a technique of printing onto felt, dyeing and
sewing the material and developing new ways of combining this into
jewellery. She is beginning to merge the two subjects by applying her
jewellery training and mindset with her love of textiles materials and
textile processes. These earrings allow O'Kelly to print pattern onto paper

Above: Angela O'Kelly, *Mixed Media Earrings*, peridots, plastic, printed felt, nylon, paper and wire, left 2.25 cm, right 4 cm × 3 cm, 2004. Photograph by Angela O'Kelly.

and felt, and to present them as a little, wearable work of art by sandwiching the filling between two thin sheets of Perspex®. The earrings are then adorned with semi-precious stones and wisps of dyed nylon filament, to create extremely tangible objects. As with much of her one-of-a-kind work, O'Kelly does not attempt to make a standard pair. She gives this option to the wearer, who chooses the balance of large with small, and the exquisite detail enhanced with areas of colour.

O'Kelly recognizes the importance of her knowledge of jewellery techniques, and these skills that are second nature to her. Perhaps most significant is the jeweller's mentality, an obsession with detail. This she exploits, setting her work apart from that of textile artists attempting to combine their craft with jewellery. O'Kelly's work will always have an edge, because she understands the fundamental rules of construction and application. She is trained to pay attention to detail, and therefore will put the appropriate emphasis on finish and fittings.

While O'Kelly prefers to work towards exhibitions, making collections that are mainly one-of-a-kind, she also produces limited edition earrings.

Above: Angela O'Kelly, *Earring Selection*, fabric paper, paper, sterling silver and wire, 1998 to 2004. Photograph by Angela O'Kelly.

The earrings shown above are made up of numerous little stamped-out paper discs, strung onto a central wire. The variety and range is endless, colour, length and form all allowing O'Kelly to play around with notions and ideas. Future thoughts are to explore scale and to produce jewellery that is not necessarily very wearable, possibly transgressing the boundaries between applied and fine art. Whatever she decides to do will certainly be interesting, and undoubtedly colourful.

Scale and colour are also important to **KIRSTIE WILSON**; throughout her degree course at Central Saint Martins College of Art & Design, it was crucial for her to learn and perfect techniques as well as exploring and relaxing her previous, rather intricate style. In her final year, Wilson specialised in enamelling, using it for colour and texture. This developed her desire to use pattern, and to further this she began to explore etching.

Wilson collects found objects and takes a great interest in 'pieces of rubbish' – scraps of nature, coins, tiny things that are old and eroded. She chooses to work in base metals such as iron, tin and mild steel, for their ageing and changing properties, enamelling straight onto the steel

Above: Kirstie Wilson, *Blue Curlicue*, consists of separate spirals of interlocking tin, 2004. Photograph by Adrian Seah.

to create the desired effect. The work shown here and on p.129 (opposite) is a theatrical extravaganza consisting of three flat spirals made out of tin, which slot together to make one piece. This is a large piece, with the main spiral measuring 25cm in length and 12cm wide, fitting over the ear, with the ear sitting inside the centre of the spiral. Each piece is painted with bright, tropical blue emulsion paint, with orange highlight details, then heated to give a bubbly texture.

Wilson has designed this piece to be worn with a dramatic yet simple costume, the one complementing the other. Her job as a dresser for the English National Ballet is a wonderful resource in terms of moving in relevant circles, and also for increasing her knowledge of costumes, props and set design. Added to this is her interest in fairy tales and fantasy, the exciting dark characters that lurk in the background of our imaginations.

Right: Kirstie Wilson, *Blue Curlicue,* on model. A whorl of joyful tropical colour curling intimately around the ear. Photograph by Adrian Seah.

If Wilson's work is about the monstrosities of the subconscious, then **REBECCA MCEVOY**'s jewellery is about challenge – the confrontation of our responses as we attempt to comprehend how little bits of dead animal have been allotted the status of a jewel. The connotations are manifold, from the initial shock and realisation of what the earring is made from, to the contemplation of a piece being worn, first by a model, then oneself! In the piece shown overleaf, a simple metal ear wire is attached to a metal circlet from which twenty-five mice tails dangle.

McEvoy uses various contacts and sources for the supply of her raw materials. Mice and rats are collected for their tails and claws, and rabbit faces for soft sections of fur. McEvoy also searches the Internet and

Left: Rebecca McEvoy, *Domestic, Wild, Pet or Vermin* ... on model. Photograph by Rebecca McEvoy.

scours antique fairs and charity shops for old fur coats and garments; she finds it hard to describe exactly what it is she is looking for, saying that she knows when she sees it.

It is vital that McEvoy achieves an end result that looks old and faded with time; her choice of materials is crucial, and attention to detail is paramount. Several simple techniques are involved in the making of a key piece such as this. First, McEvoy cuts off the mice tails with pliers and leaves them to dry out. As each tail looses moisture, it shrivels and becomes 'boney'; it does not crack, but is quite fragile, with the fur remaining intact. McEvoy then joins the tails together with thread and metal, binding and tying as necessary, then soldering the required fittings. She sources antique thread to give a natural, faded, old look. Any silver is lightly oxidised to give a browning tarnish that signifies decay, as if the piece has been around for decades, not made recently.

Performance is a means of reaching new and/or appropriate audiences, **SIMON FRASER** is a jeweller who uses this to great effect. Rather like an alchemist, Fraser takes all manner of ideas, materials and media, processing them into a very special experience. As Course Director of *MA by Project* at Central Saint Martins College of Art & Design, he is in an enviable position, able to make/involve contacts enabling him to pursue these exciting projects. Fraser aims to open up and widen the boundaries that we traditionally place jewellery within. During the performance of *Tremblante* at the Victoria and Albert Museum, London in 2001, he increased scale to vast extremes and introduced live sound with a specially composed score and by attaching microphones to jewellery.

Tremblante, meaning movement, incorporated his interest in tricks, puzzles and mechanisms, his love of exploration and the idea of transformation. The starting point was the architecture of a building, and the flat, graphic quality of plan and elevation drawings. All the work was cut out of thin sheets of nylon by hand, using various cutting implements. The act of cutting fascinates Fraser, the metamorphosis that occurs as the material is cut into, making it peel, distort and change.

Fraser succeeded in creating spectacularly large volumes, some 3.5 m long (see image overleaf). Like Christmas decorations, these earrings came to life when lifted up from their flat dormant state, stretching, hanging, huge rather extreme, quivering things. Eight models, six main and two subsidiaries, all over 20 stone in weight, were stripped down to the waist and their faces and bodies painted white except for black 'panda' eyes. Everything was scripted and planned, down to the smallest detail: the lighting structured in relationship to the jewellery iconograph, the floor area was split into formal areas, calculated mathematically, with the performers and jewellery moving between these spaces. This jewellery, so long in preparation and creation, like an insect peaked during the performance, afterwards returning to its dormant state.

Twelve months in organisation and planning, the twenty-minute performance was watched by 1,400 people on a dark, wet Friday night. While Fraser modestly insists that the stars were the earrings, one has to agree that it takes someone with motivation and a strong belief in their art to achieve a turn-out like that – never before had the British public been known for getting so excited about a few pairs of earrings!

Left: Simon Fraser, *Fat Boy Wearing Black Earrings*, nylon, ear fitting, 3.5 m long, 2001.
Photograph by Nazarin Montag.

Conclusion

Individual perceptions of value have always intrigued me. This has been constant throughout my career; when first running my own business designing and making both precious and acrylic jewellery; and even more so dealing with the very discerning Contemporary Applied Arts (CAA) clientele when I was in charge of jewellery exhibitions and gallery sales.

We are all familiar with the emotional attachment an inherited pair of earrings, or necklace or brooch can have. Many of the commissions I handled at CAA were seen by the customer as something to pass on to future generations. The piece, though designed and made by the jeweller, was the collaboration between artist and client, having an essence of the latter's taste, design input and metal/stone/material choice contained within it. A unique piece was created that was extremely personal and therefore all the more precious.

Researching and writing this book has reinforced attitudes to value in many ways. Customers are drawn to buy jewellery that excites, fascinates and has a purpose. This might simply be to wear but more often it will have the potential to have meaning. This must be why so many people choose to design and make jewellery.

Health and Safety

There are many safety considerations to take into account when making jewellery, and you should always remember your workshop training and follow any manufacturers' safety guidelines when working with materials and equipment. Equipment should always be used with due care and attention, and should be well maintained. The workshop should be well ventilated and all work areas should be kept tidy and clean. Clothing must always be kept tidy, with any apron strings, scarves, long sleeves, bracelets, long earrings, etc., removed, tied back or avoided altogether in the workshop. Be especially cautious about this when using a polishing wheel. Likewise, you should tie back long hair.

When using a polishing machine with a revolving mop, always use both hands to hold your work. Remember that a polishing machine is not the only way to polish your work – other means may be just as suitable and will probably be safer. If you are using a polishing machine to polish a thin strip of metal or a piece of wire, you should support it on a piece of wood or metal, and if using a machine to polish thin wire or a chain you should wrap this around something like the head of a mallet or a piece of plastic pipe for support. Always keep a tight grip on anything you are polishing.

Safety goggles/face visor should always be worn when polishing, soldering, engraving, or using machinery and you should always use tweezers to handle hot pieces and when you are using acids. All work areas should be kept tidy and free from obstructions, and you should only work in well-ventilated areas.

If you use acids, you should wear full safety clothing (solid footwear, safety goggles/face visor, safety apron and safety gloves) and must only work in specialist supervised facilities with full ventilation. Using nitric acid is extremely dangerous and should be avoided; if you do decide to use it, you must be sure not to inhale any vapours, wear full safety clothing and remember it is extremely corrosive. Store any chemicals in suitable containers (glass or plastic) safely out of reach of children, clearly labelled and away from heat and direct sunlight. Acids should always be disposed of safely, in accordance with local authority guidelines. Remember, only ever add acid to water, never water to acid. Keep baking soda (sodium bicarbonate) on hand to neutralise any accidental spillages.

Suggested further reading

STUDIO JEWELLERY

Cartlidge B., Twentieth-Century Jewelry, H N Abrams Inc, New York, 1985

Dormer, P. & Turner, R., The New Jewelry, Thames and Hudson, 1985

Drutt English. H. & Dormer, P., Jewelry of Our Time, Thames and Hudson, 1995

Falk, F., Schmuck der Moderne 1960-1998, Arnoldsche, 1999

Game, A. & Goring, E. Jewellery Moves, NMS Publishing, 1998

Hinks, P., Twentieth Century British Jewellery 1900-1980, Faber and Faber, 1983

Hughes, G., The Art of Jewelry – A Survey of Craft and Creation, Studio Vista, 1972

Katz S., Classic Plastics, Thames and Hudson, 1984

Katz S., Plastics – Designs and Materials, Studio Vista, 1978

Lambert, S., The Ring, RotoVision, 1998

Lewin, S. G., American Art Jewelry Today, Thames and Hudson, 1994

Turner, R., Jewelry in Europe and America, Thames and Hudson, 1996

Walgrave, J., The Ego Adorned, 20 Century Artists Jewellery, 2000

TECHNICAL BOOKS

Curtis, L., Electroforming, A&C Black, 2004

McCreight, T., Boxes and Lockets – metalsmithing techniques, A&C Black

McGrath J., Basic Jewellery Making Techniques, Headline

Murphy, K., Resin Jewellery, A&C Black

Olver E., The Art of Jewelry Design, Quarto, 2002

Olver E., The Jewellery Directory of Shape and Form, Quarto, 2000

Untracht O., Jewelry Concepts and Technology, Hale, London, 1982

Untracht O., Metal Techniques for Craftsmen, Hale, London, 1969

BUSINESS

Design Trust, Business Start-up Guide for Designers and Makers, Design Trust, 2005

Contacts: addresses and websites

SUPPLIERS AND GALLERIES

UK
The Alexander Gallery, Brighton; www.thealexandergallery.co.uk
Avant Garde, Padstow and Truro; www.avantgardejewellery.co.uk
Contemporary Applied Arts, London; www.caa.org.uk
Crafts Council, London; www.craftscouncil.org.uk
Crafts Council Shop at the V&A, London;
   www.craftscouncil.org.uk/ Trading/index.html
Electrum, London; Tel +44 (0) 20 7629 6325
Goodman Morris, Brighton; www.goodmanmorris.com
Inuti, Windsor; www.inutijewellery.co.uk
Jane Moore, Leamington Spa; www.janemoorejewellery.co.uk
Jess James, London; www.jessjames.com
Kath Libbert Jewellery, Saltaire; www.saltsmill.org.uk
Lesley Craze, London; www.lesleycrazegallery.co.uk
Malcolm Betts, London; www.malcolmbetts.com
New Ashgate Gallery, Farnham; www.newashgategallery.co.uk
Polka Dot, Exeter; www.polkadotgallery.com
The Scottish Gallery, Edinburgh; www.scottish-gallery.co.uk

HOLLAND
Galerie Louis Martin, Delft
Galerie Louise Smit, Amsterdam; www.louisesmit.nl
Galerie Marzee, Nijmegen; www.marzee.nl
Galerie Ra, Amsterdam; www.galerie-ra.nl

FRANCE
Galerie Helene Poree, Paris; www.galerie-helene-poree.fr

PORTUGAL
Galerie Reveso, Lisbon.

CANADA
Galerie Noel Guyomarc'h, Montreal; Tel +1 514 840 9362

USA
Adair Margo Gallery, El Paso, TX; www.adairmargo.com
Andora, Carefree, AZ; www.andoragallery.com
Charon Kransen Arts, New York, NY; www.charonkransenarts.com
Helen Drutt Gallery, Philadelphia, PA; Tel +1 215 735 1625
Jewelers Werk, Washington DC; Tel +1 202 293 0249
Julie Artisans' Gallery, New York, NY; www.julieartisans.com
Mobilia Gallery, Cambridge, MA; www.mobilia-gallery.com
Velvet da Vinci, San Francisco; www.velvetdavinci.com

SHOWS

UK
Dazzle, Edinburgh, Glasgow, London and Manchester;
   www.dazzle-exhibitions.com
Goldsmiths Fair, London, (October); www.thegoldsmiths.co.uk/events/
Origin, London, (October); www.craftsonline.org.uk
Pulse, London (May); www.pulse-london.com
Top Drawer, London (January and September); www.topdrawer.co.uk

USA
SOFA, Chicago (November); www.sofaexpo.com
SOFA, New York (June); www.sofaexpo.com

ARTISTS

www.craftscouncil.org.uk/photostore
www.designnation.co.uk
www.metalcyberspace.com/artists.htm
www.whoswhoingoldandsilver.com

GALLERIES

www.metalcyberspace.com/galleries.htm
www.snagmetalsmith.org/infocentral/galleries.asp

JEWELLERS – INDIVIDUAL SITES

Jane Adam: www.janeadam.com
Zoe Arnold: www.zoearnold.com
Holly Belsher: www.hollybelsher.co.uk
Malcolm Betts: www.malcolmbetts.com
Elizabeth Bone: www.elizabethbone.co.uk
Barbara Christie: www.barbarachristie.com
Katie Clarke: www.katieclarke.co.uk
Alan Craxford: www.alancraxford.com
Michael De Nardo: www.michaeldenardo.com
Mikala Djorup: www.djorup.net
Rachel Dorris: www.racheldorris.co.uk
Amanda Doughty: www.amandadoughty.com
Katy Hackney: www.katyhackney.com
Daniella Kerner:
    www.temple.edu/crafts/public_html/mjcc/local/history/p88.html
Daphne Krinos: www.daphnekrinos.com
Shaun Leane: www.shaunleane.com
Stanley Lechtzin:
    www.temple.edu/crafts/public_html/mjcc/bios/bio_lechtzin.html
Malcolm Morris: www.malcolm-morris.com
Grainne Morton: www.grainnemorton.co.uk

Mark Nuell: www.marknuell.com
Louise O'Neill: www.louise-oneill.com
Karen Robertson: www.diversegallery.com
Kayo Saito: www.kayosaito.com
Vickie Sedman:
    www.temple.edu/crafts/public_html/mjcc/bios/bio_sedman.html
Maria Spanou: www.mariaspanou.com
Scott Wilson: www.scottwilson.com

PHOTOGRAPHERS

Tim Brightmore: www.timbrightmore.co.uk
Sophie Broadbridge: www.coochie-management.com
Paul Hartley: www.hartleystudios.co.uk
Graham Lees: www.grahamlees.com
Kevin Nicholson: www.kevinnicholson.com
Michael Taylor: www.michaeltaylor.biz

Glossary of terms

Acrylic term used to describe various sheet plastics and epoxy resins.

Aluminium a soft, lightweight pale grey metal, non-corrosive.

Anodise an electrical current is passed through the metal (aluminium) to create a porous layer into which colour (dye) is absorbed.

Argentium an alloy with extra spring and hardness developed by Peter Johns.

Baguette a cut stone that is rectangular in shape.

Batch production term used when small amounts of a particular design are repeated.

Bezel setting consisting of a simple band or collar of metal surrounding a stone.

Brilliant cut has 57 facets, 33 on the crown and 25 on the pavilion, radiating out from the centre of the stone to maximise brilliance.

Briolette a cut teardrop-shaped stone.

Cabochon a domed or rounded shape of stone, with no facets.

CAD computer aided design.

CAM computer aided manufacture.

Carving reducing metal or non-precious material by filing (by hand) or using mechanised burrs to create the desired form.

Casting a mass-production process that involves pouring metal or resin into a mold.

Cellulose acetate a type of plastic, manufactured in rigid sheets of varying colours and patterns.

Cement fondualusions, glass, semi-precious stone chippings etc. This can then be ground to the desired shape/form.

Chenier another term for metal tubing.

Copper a soft, red/brown coloured base metal.

Electroforming a process used to create a layer of metal over a model or object by way of electrolysis.

Enamel a means to introduce colour by fusing glass onto metal, usually in a small kiln.

Enamel paint produced for use/ decoration in model making etc.

Engrave the application of decoration onto metal using tools called gravers.

Epoxy resin is used for casting resin into a mold; in its liquid state it is mixed with a catalyst to harden into a solid synthetic.

Etching a means of decoration by removing parts of the metal's surface using acids, covering or 'stopping-out' areas that are to remain.

Fabricate the construction of form, often hollow, from sheet and wire.

Facet the cuts of a gemstone.

Filigree decorative, delicate wire work.

Findings term used to describe the various fittings such as ear wires, brooch catches, jump links etc. used to connect jewellery together and to person/clothing.

Firestain oxide that occurs below the surface of sterling silver when it is heated, to restore the silver to its 'true' colour the firestain must be removed by filing.

Forging hammering of metal to create shape and form.

Formica® decorative laminate manufactured by Formica Limited.

Gemstone general term to describe both precious and semi precious stones.

Germanium silver a recently developed alloy that is firestain/ tarnish resistant, by Peter Johns.

Gold, 24 carat pure gold.

Gold, 22 carat 22 out of 24 parts gold, a rich yellow/red in colour.

Gold, 18 carat 18 out of 24 parts gold, the other 6 parts are made up of other metals to give different 'colours' of gold.

Gold, 9 carat 9 out of 24 parts gold, giving scope for a wide range of 'colours' of gold.

Gold plate a thin layer or coating of gold applied to the surface of silver or a base metal.

Heat form a process of heating sheet plastic (Perspex) to enable bending and forming to take place, as the plastic cools it hardens retaining the shape.

Inclusion flaws in a precious or semi-precious stone, classed as an 'imperfect' stone; many studio jewellers choose stones with inclusions for their lively and exciting sparkle.

Inlay where one metal or material is inserted into another by way of grooves or pierced shapes to give a decorative pattern.

Kumihimo a specialised Japanese braiding technique.

Laser cut sheet metal, plastic or leather etc. 'cut' to the desired shapes by way of the laser cutting along the drawn pattern on the surface of the material, done by laser specialists.

Laser weld the joining of two metal edges by fusing or welding together to become one metal using a specialist laser, no solder is used.

Limited edition a series of work where each piece is individually numbered i.e. number 3 of 25; once the series is complete it will not be repeated.

Mold a form into which molten metal or liquid resin is poured (or cast) and allowed to harden. This can be used numerous times to produce large numbers (or copies) of the original design.

Non-precious material anything other than platinum, gold or silver.

'One off' or **'One of a kind'** a term for a unique piece of work.

Opaque will not let light pass though.

Oxidisation the blackening of metal (usually silver) by using chemicals.

Palladium a silver/white metal, that looks like platinum.

Parrot tail feathers the feathers in Shaun Leane's earrings are the result of natural feather shedding and were collected over a controlled period of time.

Patination the colouring of metal by using specific chemicals to give certain colours.

Pavé setting gives the impression of the area being encrusted with stones by setting a number of small stones closely together.

Perspex® cast and extruded acrylic sheet, available in a wide range of colours.

Platinum the most precious of metals, its' value surpasses that of 24 carat gold; it is silver/white in colour, inert and therefore does not tarnish.

Plywood board made-up of thin layers of wood sandwiched together.

Polyester thread a strong synthetic thread.

Precious metals term used to describe platinum, gold and silver.

Precious stones term used to describe diamonds, emeralds, rubies and sapphires.

Production run work that is produced in large amounts or runs of a design.

Refractory metal term used to describe titanium, tantalum and niobium.

Resin *see* epoxy resin.

Reticulation occurs when metal is heated to almost melting point and the surface begins to stretch and crinkle.

Rolling by feeding metal through rolling mills its thickness can be reduced and/or pattern/texture 'rolled' onto the surface of the metal.

Rose cut this 'old fashioned' cut imitates a rose bud's petals; the base of the stone is flat with the facets meeting at a central point of the domed shaped crown.

Satin finish a matt finish achieved by a final 'papering' in one direction with a grade 1,200 wet & dry paper.

Semi-precious stone term used to describe stones such as aquamarine, citrine, iolite, tourmaline etc.

Silver, Britannia silver that is at least 95% pure.

Silver, sterling silver that is at least 92.5% pure.

Soldering where metals are joined by an alloy (solder) that melts/flows at a lower temperature than the metals it is joining.

Stainless steel contains a minimum of 12% chromium and is resistant to corrosion.

Stud also referred to as earring post.

Translucent light is allowed to pass through, but is diffussed.

Transparent light is allowed to pass through resulting in total clarity.

Index